PRAISE FOR DR. RUTH

"Her energy level is higher than that of a charged particle."

—People

"[Dr. Ruth's] manner is down-to-earth and reassuring . . . She tries to make people feel better, value themselves, and trust their instincts."

—Ladies' Home Journal

"Dr. Ruth writes the way she talks—enthusiastically, nonjudgmentally, and informatively."

—Booklist

"Her name and the distinctive thrill of her voice have become inextricably linked with the subject of sex."

—New York Times

From You to Two

From You to Two

Dr. Ruth's Rules for Real Relationships

DR. RUTH K. WESTHEIMER

WITH PIERRE A. LEHU

amazonpublishing

Published by Amazon Publishing, New York

www.apub.com

Amazon, the Amazon logo, and Amazon Publishing are trademarks of Amazon.com, Inc., or its affiliates.

ISBN-13: 9781542046725
ISBN-10: 1542046726

Cover design by Faceout Studio, Spencer Fuller

Printed in the United States of America

"It is not good for people to be alone."

—*Genesis 2: 18*

CONTENTS

INTRODUCTION

A relatively well-known French saying goes: *Plus ça change, plus c'est la même chose.* It means the more things change, the more they stay the same. No doubt the activity we call dating has undergone some enormous changes. And yet, despite those changes, dating hasn't changed all that much, because at its most fundamental level it's still boy meets girl (or boy meets boy or girl meets girl, which I suppose is indicative of one of the changes that has occurred). Ultimately, dating is a search for that basic chemical reaction between two people that either happens or doesn't, no matter the route that the two people took to find themselves sharing the same petri dish.

One point I want to make in this book is that although the new methods of dating have a lot going for them, the old methods haven't lost their value. After all, people have successfully used the old methods for quite some time. Since the goal of finding a significant other hasn't changed, if you're hitting a brick wall using the newer dating systems, then turning to some of the time-tested methods wouldn't be a bad idea.

To date successfully you need to have a goal in the first place. I don't see the point of dating just to date. Dating, as I see it, is a step toward an end—possibly marriage but at least a long-term relationship. I don't consider one-night stands, regardless of whether you have sex, a date, any more than I label an evening out with your best friend a date. A date, as I'm using the term in this book, implies that the potential for a romantic relationship exists.

I want everyone to have a rich social life. It concerns me that there are people who veg out in front of the TV for days on end or play video games all night long. Nevertheless, helping people get out and about is a subject of another book. In these pages, the main issue I'm going to address is the difficulty that many people today seem to have going from a first date to a committed relationship. If dating is, in part, a pruning process, every first date couldn't possibly lead to a long-term relationship. But when someone goes on dozens, maybe even hundreds of dates and they all wind up as dead ends, then that person needs help, and that's where I come in.

Blaming the other party for a bad date is easy. No doubt some dates that turn out badly are 100 percent the fault of one person, and most of the time that person isn't you. But more often than not, you each share some of the blame. That doesn't necessarily mean that if you had better dating techniques at your disposal and put in more effort, that one fruitless date could have been salvaged. Certainly two people might just be incompatible, and there's nothing either one of you could have done to further the relationship. But if you never shoulder any of the responsibility for dates that don't yield anything, then you won't learn anything from them. At the least every bad date should be a learning experience. Never forget that you agreed to go out with this person, so you can't be held completely blameless. Let this book lead to some critical thinking on your part, and what I've written will increase in its value. Dating is an art form, and even if you don't do it perfectly, at least you can improve your skill set.

To help you better absorb the lessons I offer in this book, I'm going to use two ways of emphasizing certain points. The first I've labeled **"Stop and Consider."** Think of these as a form of highlight to mark where I am underlining a particular point. Stop reading when you encounter one of them, and consider how what I've said applies to you. Doing so will add significant value to the experience of reading this book. (I started out as a kindergarten teacher and later taught at Yale, Princeton, Columbia, and West Point, among other colleges, so I know a thing or two about getting my students/readers to better absorb what I'm teaching.)

The other device I use to emphasize important text are tweets. These aren't actual tweets from my Twitter feed, though I might use some of them when the book is published, but as with the Stop and Considers, they are points that I want to stress, so in a sense, they're a repetition of something I just said or am about to say. If some make you smile, so much the better, because as Jewish teaching says, a lesson taught with humor is one retained.

Amusing tweets or not, I want to close this introduction by saying that I fully understand how serious the issue of dating is. It's not an activity to trivialize because the consequences are so important. A long dry dating spell can be depressing. A series of bad dates can badly shake your confidence. Someone stuck on a negative dating path could end up missing out on much of the joy that life can provide. Society tends to poke fun at the dating process—picture those TV ads you've undoubtedly seen for dating services that feature really bad dates—but an endless string of bad dates is anything but humorous. In this book I'm going to take a serious look at what you can do to improve your prospects and take the drama out of dating.

1.

What Are Your Dating Goals?

Why is developing a set of goals regarding dating so important? The simple answer is that without goals, in dating or anything else you set out to do, you're more likely to wander around aimlessly than to accomplish anything concrete. Goals give you a target on which to focus. Consider the following example: Picture yourself standing in an empty field, armed with a bow and arrow; the sole instruction is that you're supposed to shoot a dozen arrows. You'd probably stand there with a confused look on your face. You'd ask yourself, "In which direction am I supposed to shoot these arrows, and what am I supposed to shoot?" And if you did shoot those arrows in a helter-skelter fashion, how could you judge your performance? Put a target in that field, and the scenario changes dramatically, doesn't it? Now you have something to aim at, and you can judge whether you did well by how many of the arrows hit the target. Your set of dating goals will provide you with direction and a way of judging how you're doing.

Stop and Consider: What are your dating goals?

Goals come in two flavors: short-term and long-term goals. Short-term goals can often help you achieve long-term goals, but only if you've identified the long-term goal and then coordinate the two. Otherwise, a short-term goal could send you in the wrong direction.

To be successful at dating means that you have to not only choose a set of goals, but also choose those goals strategically. Each goal that you reach has to lead to the next one until ultimately you reach your final goal. Let's agree that your long-term goal is to find a steady partner, if not a spouse. If your primary short-term goal is to have a date next Saturday night, and you're willing to accept just about any date that comes along just so that you can announce to your friends on Facebook that you won't be sitting home alone, then even if you successfully meet that goal, you might not be making any progress toward your long-term goal. By worrying about what your friends might think about you being dateless on Saturday, you're putting pressure on yourself, which means that you're likely to offer or accept a date invitation from someone whose long-term prospects verge on nil. The same holds true if this pressure is coming from your mom, your coworkers, or your teenage children. Your time would be better spent trying to find that one special person than going out solely for the sake of not staying home.

Dates that come about because you're giving in to some sort of societal pressure are rarely productive. I'm not going to say they are *never* productive, because that date made out of desperation for next Saturday night could be that one in a million, but your odds significantly improve if the reason you're going on a date with someone is based on the simple fact that this other person appeals to you rather than he or she just fills the void.

<u>Stop and Consider:</u> When you agree to a date, do you make sure that the person fits with your long-term goals?

What if the pressure to date is coming from loneliness? Is that an excuse to take any date that comes your way? I'd say yes only if you haven't had a date in an extremely long time. Dating is a skill, and if you're out of practice, when the time comes for a date that has potential, you want to be in the best possible form. So I'm not against "practice dating." But practice dating isn't dating any more than hitting a tennis ball back and forth to warm up is a game of tennis. You can't lose, but you also can't win.

However, you can lose at some forms of practice dating. I consider friends with benefits (FWB) dates to be in that category. Although I'm not saying that two people can't have casual sex, casual sex that takes place on a regular basis between the same two people eventually might not be casual for one of the people involved in such a relationship. Developing romantic interest in a FWB partner can lead to heartbreak. Then what often happens is that the person with the romantic interest will continue to see the other on a FWB basis just to spend time with the object of his or her desire, not even hinting that his or her feelings have changed so as not to scare away this "friend."

There's always a risk that if two people regularly spend a lot of time together that one might develop unreciprocated feelings for the other. That risk greatly increases when sex is added to the mix. In fact, baring both your body and emotions can't help but bring you closer, so I recommend not becoming that intimate with anybody until you both have developed feelings for each other beyond a vague friendship. There's certainly no guarantee that waiting to have sex until some time has passed will protect you from heartbreak, but a waiting period will reduce the odds of your heart being torn in two.

Furthermore, a FWB date or hook-up date is unlikely to further your long-term goal. How can you possibly meet your future romantic partner if you're having sex with someone who you know doesn't fit your requirements for a committed relationship, or who doesn't think that you fit his or her serious relationship profile? In such cases your short-term goal, having sex with a warm body, is detracting you from your long-term goal.

Earlier I said that there's nothing wrong with casual sex or hooking up. By that I meant that I wasn't inserting a moral message and calling it a sin. But my statement about casual sex does need some clarification. First, you have to consider the issue of safety, in terms of sexually transmitted infections, unintended pregnancy, and personal safety. Casual sex carries risks in all these categories. Hence, having casual sex becomes a personal decision of whether its pleasure outweighs the risks. If alcohol or drugs are involved, then the word *decision* needs to be in quotes, because what you agree to under the influence of one of these substances might not be an activity that you'd agree to if you were sober.

Whether or not you read these next few paragraphs, my conscience obliges me to include them. Condoms may not provide sufficient protection against a sexually transmitted infection (STI). HIV/AIDS may be the scariest STI because it's the deadliest, but some of the most prevalent diseases can infect you without you ever knowing about it. You don't get any symptoms, until you discover later on that, for example, you're unable to have children because an STI rendered you infertile. I know that scare tactics don't work, but don't ignore these dangers, and if you do engage in casual sex, always use protection. (Keep in mind that condoms aren't a 100 percent guarantee of safe sex.)

An unintended pregnancy can occur with any heterosexual partner, because condoms can break or slip off, but casual sex is sometimes so relaxed that you or your partner might not even use a condom. Even sterilization (like a vasectomy) has failed in some instances, so no form of birth control is 100 percent guaranteed to prevent an unintended pregnancy. Because the risk of an unintended pregnancy always exists with sexual intercourse between men and women, I urge you to think twice or even three times before engaging in casual sex. (Oral and anal sex do protect you from an unintended pregnancy, but both leave you susceptible to STIs.)

I'll address personal safety more when discussing online dating (see chapter 3), but here I want to mention a type of danger to your privacy. With everybody posting to Facebook or other social media all their day's activities, you can be pretty sure that if you go out on a date with someone, some or all of the details will show up online. If the date goes well, that may not matter, but if this person took a dislike to you or is just a bit off and dislikes everybody, then he or she may post nasty things about you. What this person posts might be untrue, but the nasty words will be out there for many people to read. Even worse consequences could develop if you end up having sex with a date who takes pictures or videos of you in some compromising position, whether surreptitiously or with your permission, and then posts them. There's no telling where those pictures will wind up and what harm they may do to your personal life and business career. Could a lover or even spouse do this to you as well as a casual date? You bet, which is why I'd be very cautious when it comes to posing nude under any circumstances. You've seen pictures on the internet of celebrities having sex; surely those celebrities were certain the pictures would remain private. But without a doubt, someone you barely know will have fewer scruples about posting nude pictures online, and in fact might have been seeking that particular thrill in the first place. And by the way, just because you don't see any cameras doesn't mean there aren't any.

Everybody tries to paint themselves in the best light on their online bio, but many people take a few steps over that line or maybe even many steps. When you first meet someone, you don't know how much this person has exaggerated the truth, which is one reason why I urge extra caution until you know someone you've been chatting with a lot better.

<u>Stop and Consider:</u> Can you fully trust someone who lies or exaggerates on his or her online profile?

You're probably familiar with the phrase "too good to be true." That's why the better the profile of the person you're about to date is, the more careful I advise you to be. You've undoubtedly received e-mails from Nigeria in which someone supposedly has an account with $50 million that he wants to share with you, and you know those are a scam in part because they're so exaggerated. But those e-mails wouldn't be sent out if the senders didn't occasionally cause someone to part with some hard-earned money. The same goes with people, both men and women, who paint an amazing portrait of themselves to lure in unsuspecting victims.

To some degree, dating is like a Google search. You know this other person's name and a few other details from what was posted online, and now your goal is to open the box, i.e. date, to find out what's inside that packaging, or at least that may be your goal. Some people, mostly men, unfortunately have only one goal: to have sex with as many women as possible. After they've achieved their goal with a particular woman, they're ready to move on. (And gay men looking for a romantic relationship may face the same issue.) Even if they stick around for a while, enjoying the sex, at whatever point their eyes lock on some new target, they're gone. For the most part, dating is a step-by-step process during which you learn more about each other and decide whether to continue dating or not.

For my readers who are wondering how to spot these one-track-minded gentlemen, I'm afraid that I don't have any easy answers, but I can tell you that if you're seeking a relationship and not just casual sex, make a point of never having sex on the first date. Many of these men seeking only sex will disappear if they're not successful on the first try, and so at least you won't be wasting any more time with one of these would-be Casanovas whom you happen to date.

Running into this kind of man is one of the pitfalls of selecting your dates from some website or app. If a man comes with a personal recommendation that he's looking for a relationship, then you can probably trust that. But if he wrote down such intentions himself on a description, it could easily be a lie.

And then there are the men who aren't sure themselves. If the right woman came along, they might be willing to have a real relationship, but if a date yields nothing more than sex, that's all right with them too. In such cases, my advice about not having sex right away stands and maybe is even reinforced. Because if he likes the woman, then maybe he'll stick around and with time decide that he'd enjoy a relationship. But if he gets sex right away, before he's made up his mind, then he might be less inclined to continue dating you.

Am I discriminating against men here? To some extent, because I know that some women are certainly looking for nothing more than sex as well. However, in the dating scene, men interested in sex greatly outnumber women interested only in sex. One reason is that men are more likely to have a satisfying sexual experience without any romantic feelings attached to the act while fewer women can say the same. I'm fully cognizant that many women can have very satisfying casual sex, but many can't. Physically speaking, women typically need more time to become fully aroused than men, but in addition, without some romance, some emotional quotient, many women just can't become sufficiently sexually aroused to have an orgasm. Since time immemorial men have been going to prostitutes for sexual satisfaction, so it seems that, for men, sexual satisfaction can be a commodity that can be purchased without the need for any romantic attachment.

Dangers do exist, but keeping your goal in mind during this exploration process can provide some protection. Although idle curiosity might drive you to open up an app and flip through pictures, that shouldn't be the case when spending several hours of your life with someone. What should always be in the back of your mind when dating is the possibility that you could end up spending the rest of your life with this person you currently barely know.

Dr. Ruth Westheimer ✓
@AskDrRuth

Choosing whom to date should be like choosing which movie to see. Pick the one with the best ratings, not just any movie listed at the multiplex.

For you to appreciate my logic, you have to understand the value I put on time. Most people are spoiled, believing that the good times will last forever. If you had my history—if you'd lost your entire family to the Nazis, spent six years in an orphanage, joined the underground fighting for Israel's freedom in 1948, and been seriously wounded in a bomb blast where people right next to you died—you'd always have a healthy fear of what tomorrow could bring. I admit the second half of my life has been blessed in ways I never could have imagined, but those early experiences always remain with me, so I want to fill every second I've been given to the max.

<u>Stop and Consider:</u> How much time do you waste every day?

Time is your most precious resource. It's 100 percent limited, and you have no idea how much you have left in the bank. There will come a day when you'll regret the hours you wasted, which is why you're better off not wasting them to begin with. I'm not saying that dating without any interest in romance can't be fun. It most certainly can be, but finding someone to love and being loved is so much better that you should make it your goal and not postpone it.

Society may treat dating as a light and fluffy topic, but it's actually a serious one. Today many people face an epidemic of loneliness. The negative impact being alone has on people can be severe, and the spike in teenage suicide is one example. We human beings need to be in the company of other human beings, and for that human contact to be effective, it has to be reliable. Certainly family offers such human contact, but today so many people have moved away from where they grew up or where their family resides that daily or even weekly family contact isn't possible. Starting a new family by becoming part of a committed couple isn't just a luxury but rather an actual need for good psychological health, which is why most people desire to be part of a committed couple. Yes, there are times in everyone's life when they choose to be single. The reason could be situational, such as you've been assigned to a new city for a short amount of time or maybe you've experienced some painful breakups and need time to recover. But if you're reading this book, it's safe to say that you're not looking to remain single, and so the sooner you fulfill your goal to acquire a partner, the better off you'll be.

Some of you have been in longtime relationships that have ended. The reasons for the split vary—death, divorce, etc.—but your goal will be to replace that part of you that is now missing, because having a significant other is much like having a living person attached to you. Depending on how you lost your love, you may be more wary about kindling another. If you were badly hurt, not being hurt again is certainly going to be an important goal. But a fear of being hurt again mustn't keep you from dating and finding a new lover.

If you were part of a couple for many years, you undoubtedly had a lot of good times. Your job is to concentrate on those times and not allow the end of the relationship, however it came about, to influence your future. I used the word *replace*—your new lover will replace your old one, but you must separate yourself and look at this new partnership as creating a new future that is not affected by your past at all.

Is your situation different from someone still looking for that special someone? Of course, and yet you must learn to look at this search just as someone would who'd never lost a love. Your next lover won't have been a part of your old life. Having too much of an aura of the past about you will chase away the new people you meet.

Dr. Ruth Westheimer ●
@AskDrRuth

Sometimes it's best to move on even when it's not the obvious move.

If you're in the dating game and are looking for someone to love and who will love you back, my advice is to be as focused as possible on making that desire come true. Using that logic, if you're dating someone who you absolutely know isn't the type of person with whom you would want to spend the rest of your life, then move on. Better to be single and open to finding a romantic partner than filling your calendar dating someone with whom you have no future.

If you're out with friends, you're not sitting home alone, and you're also open to meeting a potential new lover. Your friends might even act as wingmen. However, if you're dating someone who doesn't meet the criteria that you've set for a permanent relationship, as long as you're with this person, you're closing yourself off to any chance encounters. Dating someone who doesn't have long-term potential is a waste of your precious time. Moving on might make you sad, but ultimately you'll be glad you did because it will bring you closer to reaching your goal.

Stop and Consider: Are you dating someone whom you know you would never consider for a serious relationship?

Because dating requires two people, one of your goals must be to meet people who share your desire for a long-term romantic relationship.

14

Deciding that someone is a match isn't a decision to make lightly, and you're not going to find someone with a sign around his or her neck that says "Long-Term Relationships Only."

When you utilize an e-dating service (and by "e-dating" I mean using either a computer program, an app on your phone, or both), many people do just that—they say they're looking for a long-term relationship. How certain can you be that because someone on a dating site says he or she is looking for a long-term partner that it's a true statement? People lie on these sites, so until you meet and get to know this person you've found online, you can't tell what his or her goal really is. Some people are just as good at lying in person as they are in writing, but it's easier to lie when you're not looking into someone's eyes. If you listen carefully, you'll note that a liar rarely limits his or her lies to just one subject. Even if it's difficult to know for sure whether this person is telling you the truth about the desire for a long-term relationship, spot a few other lies and you can be fairly certain that his or her commitment to commitment is false.

Spotting liars and the lies they tell is a talent that you have to develop if you're going to succeed in your goal. The first art you must develop if you're going to be any good at spotting liars is that of listening. Liars count on their audience not paying close attention to what they say. If they are caught, they're able to deny a lie later. When you're in the initial dating phase, you have to make sure and remember what your date said so if it proves false later on, you'll know that this other person is a liar. He or she may try to convince you otherwise by saying, "I never said that," but you'll know better.

Being a good listener requires more than paying attention to the words coming out of your date's mouth. We humans communicate in many ways, so you need to watch this other person closely when he or she is speaking. Facial expressions or body language may be saying something entirely different than the words you are hearing.

To help you improve your ability to read body language, watch someone being interviewed on TV. Instead of just being a casual observer, carefully note the facial expressions of both the host and the guest. Look at their mouths, eyes, eyebrows, forehead, etc. Notice how their body language echoes their words. Pay attention to what facial expressions signify anger, humor, honesty, etc. Then try to do the same with friends. You've been subconsciously noting these expressions your entire life. You've been reading the signals of body language since you were a baby but without realizing what you were doing. If you force yourself to be more aware of facial expressions and other body language, you'll become better at reading them. Although most people use these means of communication subconsciously, if you get more familiar with them, you can teach yourself to control your own body language better so that you communicate more effectively.

Typically when you're talking to someone in person, you may not be conscious of the different ways a face adds meaning to the words being said, but you still subconsciously absorb the information. If your instincts aren't working effectively, you're unsure what your subconscious is hinting at, or you're nervous because you're on a first date, then force yourself to pay closer attention to your date's body language. Doing so will take added concentration on your part, but if you keep your goal in mind, then the effort will be worth it.

If you're young enough, online dating sites may seem to have been around forever, but in terms of human history, they didn't exist a blink of an eye ago. On the other hand, human communications have been going on since Homo sapiens stepped out of the jungle, so baked into our genes is the need to look into somebody's eyes and study the body language of the person you're communicating with in order to understand the full meaning of what he or she is saying. Take away all that information and it's like looking at the *Mona Lisa* in a darkened room and trying to judge whether it's a fake or not.

Be warned, though, that body language isn't always accurate. For example, if police officers are grilling a criminal who is sweating, then they're probably going to assume that he or she isn't telling the truth. Just because your date may be sweating and nervous about being on a first date doesn't mean that he or she is lying. However, if an hour goes by and the two of you have gotten to know each other enough that your date's nerves should have calmed down, but suddenly your date is saying something and sweating, fidgeting, or looking anywhere but in your eyes, then you can assume that more than likely he or she is offering you a fabrication of some sort.

Of course, there's looking for a committed relationship and "looking for a committed relationship." In other words, some people may have a committed relationship as a long-term goal, but they are actually operating in the short term, so that the far-off goal does not have much weight. Dealing with this situation is tricky because on the first few dates, you're not committed to this person. But if you start to develop feelings for him or her, then you're going to be hoping that those feelings are reciprocated. What if this other person isn't ready to do so? Then he or she will hold his or her emotions under a tight rein, and you might find yourself falling for someone who isn't really available.

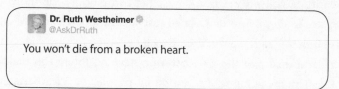

Dr. Ruth Westheimer ✓
@AskDrRuth

You won't die from a broken heart.

Falling in love is a risky business, and a lot of hearts are broken every day. Luckily you won't die from a broken heart, so you just have to accept the risks. And because it's possible that you'll be the one to break someone's heart, you just have to play the game of love to the best of your ability. I've warned you about the risks of sexually transmitted infections, unintended pregnancy, and privacy violations, because they are risks that you can protect yourself against while dating successfully.

Broken hearts, on the other hand, just come with the territory. They're a risk you just have to take, because the potential rewards are well worth it.

Ask yourself the question: How committed are you to a committed relationship? I've said that such a relationship should be your goal, but have you accepted that goal fully or partially? Maybe you're the one looking at dating as just for fun in the present, though you'd be open to meeting that special someone if he or she came along. The problem with that attitude is that you're most likely to attract others with the same outlook on dating, if not some with even less desire to commit. When you write your profile, if you indicate that although you want to be in a steady relationship you're also open to just having a good time, then how much less likely will it be that you attract others looking for commitment?

Stop and Consider: How committed are you to the idea of being in a committed relationship?

The attitude you project is a key element in guiding the individuals you date. If they sense that you're just in the mood to party, and if that's all they're looking for, then they'll be happy to date you. On the other hand, many of those people who have no interest in making a commitment are going to shy away from people who clearly state that they want a serious relationship. Most people don't want to go into a relationship knowing they're going to disappoint the other person. Not everybody, but most people.

The tricky part is that you're not offering a commitment to everyone you date. In fact, you could meet plenty of people on an app like Tinder that you won't see for a second date. How do you best communicate to the dating world that you're looking for a long-lasting relationship without seeming like a total prude or so needy that it's a turnoff?

The first part of the answer to that question has to do with you and how you feel. If you're wishy-washy about commitment, then that feeling is going to come through. Quite possibly you're not ready for a committed relationship, which is fine, but then don't go complaining that you're meeting all sorts of people not worthy of your time. The wider the net you cast, the more fish are going to get caught in it. If you indicate that you're serious about your goal of finding Mr. or Ms. Right, then many of those who only want to hook up won't bother with you.

How do you communicate that in your profile? What if your profile read something like:

> Looking for someone who wants to jump off the dating treadmill with me. Tired of having to delete vacation pictures because my past boyfriend (or girlfriend) was in them. My Uber bill is way too high, and I need someone in my life I don't have to go out to see. I love my hometown, but I'm willing to move for the right person.

Or if you really want to get your point across, you could add that you left your former boyfriend or girlfriend because he or she wouldn't commit.

And how do you phrase this attitude when you're actually on a date? Hopefully this person has read your complete profile, but you can't count on that. Some people just look at a picture and take a leap of faith after that. Or they might just skim the profile. Or they've forgotten much of what they read by the time you first meet. You can't lead off by asking someone if they're interested in a committed relationship. That would be tacky, plus you don't know the person well enough to want to raise the issue of commitment. What you can do is adopt an attitude that shows you're a serious person who isn't interested in casual hookups. Give that message in some offhand ways a couple of times and it will get across.

How do you do that? First, dress to the message. The visual message of a low-cut blouse may just blind a male date to whatever oral messages you're communicating, so cover up. Then try to be "all business." Ask a lot of questions that indicate you care about more serious issues than this person's ability to consume alcohol or play pranks. Ask what this person sees in his or her future and what plans and dreams drive him or her. Even if you've covered some of these subjects in previous chats, in person you can go deeper and get a better sense of who this person really is. And the more the topics you address concern the long term, the more obvious it will be that you're not seeking a short-term relationship. Don't be so serious that you turn the other person off; just be serious enough that he or she will understand that you aren't just looking for a good time.

But, as should be obvious: Before you can let the world know you're looking for that special someone, you have to commit to this goal fully. You're no longer a teenager who develops a crush on this classmate one day and that one the next. Someone who might share the rest of your life with you has to have all the right qualities, and to find that someone is going to take some disciplined effort on your part. Saying that you have a goal like finding a partner isn't sufficient; you have be ready to work toward that goal.

Dr. Ruth Westheimer ✓
@AskDrRuth

Don't forget that opposites attract.

A first date offers you the opportunity to size up this person you've never met in all sorts of ways. I accept that these days information is available online that might once have taken you a long time to discover on your own. (Of course, you don't have to rely entirely on what this person has posted on his or her dating profile. A quick check on Google or a closer examination of someone's Facebook page might be quite revealing.) But, to my way of thinking, the chemical reaction that takes place between two people who are in each other's presence far outweighs knowing that someone shares some of your likes and dislikes. Opposites attract as much as similarities. Getting you to believe that someone who adores sushi and *Star Wars* is a good match for you is how the dating sites make their money, but then ask some of your married and committed friends and see how many of them have only shared interests. Why are there chick flicks and guy movies? Men's magazines and women's magazines? Channels devoted to soap operas and others to sports? Yes, having things in common is vital to a relationship, but you're different people who are bound to have different interests. It would be weird if you didn't. And maybe weird if you did. (In other words, if this guy or gal on the date immediately agreed that whatever you liked, he or she liked too, that could be weird. Trying that hard to please would make me suspicious.) If you have some common ground, that's great, but there's nothing wrong with developing some common interests after you're together. It's sort of like buying ready-to-wear clothes versus bespoke, handmade outfits. Custom designed is always going to be superior.

When reading online profiles, be discriminating but not closed-minded. If someone plays the violin and you're not into classical music, appreciate that this person is musical and could teach you to appreciate music in ways you never imagined. Or if he or she isn't widely traveled and you love to travel, think how fun it might be to act as his or her tour guide in the worldwide cities you love.

Dr. Ruth Westheimer ✓
@AskDrRuth

Your core beliefs have a role to play in your dating choices.

You might have some core beliefs that you absolutely require a lifetime partner to share with you. A common one is religion. People of different religions can have a good marriage, but that doesn't mean that you will want to compromise on something this important. Sharing your life with someone of a different religion, or without religious beliefs, is likely to cause some flak with your family that you'd prefer to avoid. Furthermore, going to a religious service as a couple is more rewarding than always attending solo. If you're going to raise a family, then being of the same religion can make it easier.

Don't neglect the role of faith in your life. If you are to become a permanent couple, you're supposed to remain faithful to each other, and the stronger one's moral compass, the more likely such faithfulness will remain a part of your relationship. Faith is something that often needs shoring up. Even the most faithful person sometimes has doubts, and sharing religious services is one important way of supporting each other's faithfulness. Although being of the same religion or even being religious isn't necessary to remain faithful, sharing religious values can definitely reinforce a relationship. If this is one of your core beliefs, then don't be afraid to make sharing religion a goal.

Does that mean you only date people of your religion? It could if developing feelings for someone of another religion or no religion would put you between that rock and hard place people are always talking about. If sharing religion is a long-term goal, then why would you waste your time dating people who don't share that goal? Some individuals might put you down for only dating people of your own religion, but if doing so is important to you, then you definitely have my blessing.

Here are some other types of lines in the sand that you might want to lay down. Some famous couples have polar-opposite political views, but spending a lot of time with someone whose political views are vastly different from yours might not be the type of relationship in which you will thrive. You might tolerate moderate alcohol use but not heavy use. A drug such as marijuana, which is legal in many places, may be off limits in the relationship you want, or it might be something you want to share. On the other hand, the use of other drugs may not be acceptable to you. If you're into being healthy or not eating meat, dating someone who's into junk food and steak might be a deal killer. If you have strong beliefs and core values, then note them and make having them in common with a partner part of your goals.

Dr. Ruth Westheimer ●
@AskDrRuth

Stare into the future; if you don't like what you see as the two of you as a couple, walk away.

Whatever your beliefs, everyone wants someone who can be trusted and who is committed to your best interests. If you're dating someone who is selfish and does what he or she pleases without caring how you might feel about it, how likely is it that you're going to end up a happy couple? Avoiding someone like that is certainly a goal you should set. If the future looks bleak, then I suggest you end the relationship before it even really begins.

You probably know couples for whom fighting and maybe even abuse is the norm. Some people say they can't help but be attracted to "bad" people. To me, being attracted to someone isn't the same as fulfilling a goal. If a key aspect of your goal is happiness, then being with someone who makes you miserable is the wrong choice. And who you date is a choice. If you see signs in someone you're dating that conflict is going to be a part of life with that person, then quickly run away. Or if you're strongly attracted to this person, literally tear yourself away. This is where having a goal is extremely valuable, because it will help you to choose wisely rather than impulsively.

Stop and Consider: Do you find that you're always ending up with someone who mistreats you in some way?

You aren't fated to be with a significant other who mistreats you. For whatever reason, you might be attracted to people who have a mean streak, but if you know that, then you have to be extra careful. You might even consider going to therapy to discover whether something in your personal history is leading you to make bad choices. Recognize the possibility that your attraction to this individual may have nothing to do with that person specifically but rather with something in your past. Until you figure out how to deal with these past events, you're never going to choose wisely.

This may be a good opportunity to discuss my particular type of therapy, which is behavioral therapy as opposed to psychology or psychiatry. I'm a sex therapist, which is a type of behavioral therapist, and what those of us in this profession do is to help people change their behaviors without looking deeply at what is causing them to act in ways that they want to change. If someone comes to see me with a sexual problem that I think might be medical in nature, then I'll send him or her to see a medical doctor. A mental condition like depression is one that falls into the category that I can't fix. But if it's a typical sexual problem, like premature ejaculation or the inability to give oneself permission to have orgasms, then I'll give my client homework to help him or her overcome this behavior.

What would I suggest to a woman who came to my office complaining that she always chooses the wrong man, one who ends up hurting her? I wouldn't dig into her past to see whether she was abused as a child, because I'm not trained to do that. That type of psychotherapy can take months and even years to uncover the source of a problem like this, whereas behavioral therapy is short term. Without delving into her past and without knowing the exact cause, I can be fairly sure that the problem is based at least in part on low self-esteem. Low self-esteem leads people to feel that they aren't worthy of having someone who treats them well. I would give my client homework to help build up her self-esteem. Some of it may be physical—like going for a makeover—and some of it may be mental—like going back to school to finish a degree. And by the way, you don't have to have that degree to feel better about yourself; just knowing that you're enrolled in a program will help a lot. The same applies with weight loss. Being overweight can lower your self-esteem, but just starting a weight-loss program will raise it. By working out a program to raise my client's self-esteem and then making sure that she sticks to it, I can help her avoid accepting people into her life who will treat her badly. It's not that she couldn't do this on her own, but with my support and expertise, what seemed impossible suddenly becomes possible. Trust me, I can be persuasive!

That's not to say that someone with low self-esteem wouldn't also benefit from seeing a psychologist or psychiatrist to find out the underlying cause. That would be the individual's decision, but a behavioral therapist can help clients to make immediate progress in areas where they require help.

If you keep choosing the wrong type of person, make one of your short-term goals changing that behavior rather than saying it's inevitable. Take steps to achieve that goal and you'll be much less likely to choose the wrong person. But if you're leaving to chance who that next person will be to fall into your arms, then your laziness may come with a high price. If you feel that you can't do it on your own, seek a therapist who can help you. It's your choice whether you go to a psychologist who'll rummage around in your past or a behavioral therapist such as myself, or both, but do go for help.

<u>Stop and Consider:</u> Are you dating someone on impulse or because of a thought-out decision?

The bonds that make two people click are complex. Scientists can explain how two molecules come together, but nobody really knows why two people are attracted to each other. Physical appearance is part of the initial attraction, but if your personalities don't mesh, physical attraction won't keep you from eventually separating. So don't allow a good first impression based on physical appearance to trick you into furthering a relationship that in the end won't be a rewarding, long-lasting one. Instead, as the dating process proceeds, give careful consideration to all the qualities of this other person and make a conscious decision about whether the goals you've set for a future relationship are being met by this person.

Dr. Ruth Westheimer ✓
@AskDrRuth

Good communication is essential in a committed relationship.

How much can you tell about a person from some texts? Certainly nothing subtle is going to come through about anyone. Texts don't compare to a face-to-face meeting. Talking on the phone is a bit of an improvement, but not that much, unless you spend hours on the phone. Before you go on a date with someone you've met on a dating app, the likelihood is that all you've done is communicate on a surface level and one that takes a minimal amount of skill. And then you meet. If the person you're dating can't seem to express him or herself in person, on a one-on-one basis, that's an indication that long-term communications between the two of you could be an issue. It might be a case of jitters that will disappear after you've dated more than once or twice, and your communications could improve, but do consider how well the two of you communicate when deciding whether this person meets your long-term goal. If you two have issues communicating, then maybe this person isn't right for you.

Another problem with online interactions is the time interval between texts. You send a text, and it might be minutes, hours, or even days before you receive a reply. Sometimes you get an instantaneous answer, but often you won't. Forgetting about the concept of love at first sight, it's hard to discover a person's true self when he or she has time to think about what to write or say in an electronic response. Most of the time you and this other person carefully edit what you say so as to present the best possible impression. However, if you're sitting together having coffee and you pose a question, even if the other person pauses for a second or two before replying, it's quite likely that you'll spot a facial change that will tell you a lot. And if you've been talking awhile, you're both going to let your guard down, at least occasionally. Those moments allow you to gauge whether someone is worth pursuing. Reading an online profile that's been pored over, and maybe even professionally written, just doesn't paint a complete picture. It might be a good starting point, but you have to recognize that's all it is.

By the way, those instances in which you let your guard down are burgeoning moments of intimacy. The two of you are connecting in some way. Intimacy, like love, is an emotion that grows when nurtured. Just because you allowed a little of your true self shine through doesn't mean that you can be considered intimate, but it's a sign that the relationship is developing in the right direction. Maximizing intimacy with a lover should definitely be one of your goals. On the other hand, constantly feeling like you're on the defensive when you're with someone is a sign that perhaps you're not meant for each other.

<u>Stop and Consider:</u> Have you ever felt that moment when you let your guard down with another person? Was it the start of a meaningful relationship?

I repeat: I'm not against e-dating (though I admit that with all the cautions I'm giving you that it might sound like I am). I just want to point out the pitfalls. If online dating isn't working for you, don't give up on the more traditional methods of finding people to date. Dating is an art, not a science. When you place too much emphasis on apps and algorithms, you risk missing some important aspects of dating.

If one of your goals is to find someone to love sooner rather than later and online dating is working for you, that's great. But if it's not, then try out the more standard methods to see if you can't improve your chances.

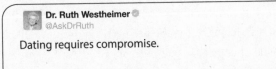

Dr. Ruth Westheimer ⊘
@AskDrRuth

Dating requires compromise.

When you first started to notice the same or opposite sex as more than just a friend, your goal might have been to land Prince Charming or a Playmate centerfold. But for the vast majority of people, these expectations are unrealistic, more so than getting straight As in school or taking a trip to Disneyland. For some people, such dreams are actually quite dangerous. Here's an example: I knew a young lady who made an appointment to see me. She had seen that Jerry Seinfeld had been on my TV show, and the purpose of her visit was to ask me to get her a date with the comedian, who, at the time, was still a bachelor.

Young men weren't beating down this young lady's door to ask her out, and yet here she was in my office, believing that because she knew me she could land this rich and famous bachelor. First of all, because someone is a guest on my show doesn't mean I know him or her. Jerry wasn't my friend. I had merely shared a stage with him for fifteen minutes. Even if I were his friend and could arrange for a blind date, I knew that such a date would never work out and would never have tried to set it up. In the Jewish tradition, making a match is a blessing, called a mitzvah, and I've made some in my life, but setting someone up for failure, which is what would have happened, is not what I would ever do.

The real problem wasn't that this young lady wanted to date Jerry Seinfeld. The problem was that she wanted to date *only* Jerry Seinfeld.

She had set her sights on this impossible target and couldn't be dissuaded. And as a result, she sat home alone every night. Her goal was too far out of reach.

Some young women decide ahead of time that they want to be a doctor's or lawyer's wife and so work toward that end. Certainly the odds of success of that goal are better than marrying a major celebrity, but so are the odds of being an unhappy doctor's or lawyer's wife because you landed someone with a degree but not a heart. If you become blinded by the title you've been seeking, then you're bound to gloss over negative attributes of this candidate, which over time might make your life miserable.

<u>Stop and Consider:</u> Are you dating someone for the wrong reason such as money, social standing, or political power?

I have rich friends who are wonderful individuals, so having money or social standing doesn't make you an awful person. But when people aren't nice and don't care for anyone other than themselves, then they aren't the type of people you want to date. Even if you manage to stick by the side of this far-from-ideal partner long enough to go down the aisle together, there's going to be a price to pay that's much higher than whatever benefits there may be from being attached.

I understand that everyone you date won't have the potential to become a future spouse. All dates are an unknown quantity until you meet them. I wouldn't want you to go to Las Vegas to elope with somebody you'd only known for a week. Spend time with someone you're introduced to and get to know that person before getting serious. However, if at any moment in this introductory period it becomes clear that you could never marry this person, and your main goal is to find someone to commit to, then end this relationship and go back to searching for someone with whom you can fall in love.

Can you move someone from the date category to the friend category, maybe even FWB category, and still keep your eye on your goal? I don't believe so. Even if in your mind he or she isn't a keeper, and even if you've informed him or her of this change in status, it's going to make it more difficult for you to have the freedom and the initiative to find someone who meets your goal if you're still seeing each other regularly. Reaching a goal isn't always easy. What is easy is calling this person you've dated but decided isn't the keeper you're looking for and saying let's go see a movie. Sometimes you need to experience the loneliness and sexual frustration of being single to force yourself to take action to change your status.

Allow me to discuss something that is rarely spoken about—masturbation—that serves as an example of my point. Nothing is wrong with masturbating to release sexual tension. I'm often asked, "How much masturbation is too much?" The answer is, "It depends." Certainly if someone is masturbating so much that it affects his or her grades in school or his ability to perform his job or maintain a social life, then that is too much. But if you're seeking a partner, then being a little sexually frustrated can be a source of impetus to get you moving in your search to find a partner. To someone having a hard time motivating him or herself to date and who is masturbating regularly, I say to cut back or even stop altogether. That subtraction may add the motivation you need.

Dr. Ruth Westheimer
@AskDrRuth

Depending on where you are in your life, masturbation may be a useful tool or a crutch that holds you back.

To some degree, dating someone who you are certain doesn't have the potential to be your long-term romantic interest is like masturbating. You're satisfying certain needs, those that stem from wanting not to be alone, but this fleeting satisfaction is actually an impediment to finding what you seek. Maybe a few lonely weekend nights are exactly the impetus required for you to force yourself to sign on to an app or take a class known to attract singles.

Dr. Ruth Westheimer ●
@AskDrRuth

Being successful isn't just about having goals but also about having the mindset to meet them.

All your goals in life need to be prioritized, because each one has an effect on the others. I can't tell you how high you should rank finding a partner, because that decision depends on many factors, such as your age, what you are currently involved in, and whether you are in school seeking a degree, starting a career, or taking care of a sick parent. But I strongly suggest that you make a list of your goals in an order of priority so that you can determine where there might be any conflicts. Because dating is a social activity, pay closer attention to your other social activities to see whether any are interfering with this goal of finding a permanent partner, which would include dating people who you are sure don't fit that category.

If you're a woman, then you've probably heard family and friends discussing your biological clock after you've passed a certain age and before you've reached menopause. Having children is an important goal, and dating is an integral part of reaching that goal. Of course, you don't necessarily need a committed partner to have a child. Plenty of single women are mothers. But having been a single mother myself, let me say that being a single mother is far from an ideal situation, especially concerning your social life, because babysitters are expensive and hard to find. This biological clock concept is one that young women should have in mind. I'm not saying that you should make a serious compromise with regard to a partner just to have a child, but if childbearing is one of your goals, see that finding the father of your child heads toward the top of your list as you start to approach that critical age when bearing children may no longer be possible.

Men can father a child at almost any age, but children aren't easy to rear. They require a lot of resources in terms of time, energy, and money. Being old enough to be retired when you're still paying tuition is going to take a toll on you, so the concept of not waiting too long to have children doesn't apply only to my female readers.

At what point you start sharing a goal like having children with someone you're dating is an important discussion. I suggest you begin looking for opportunities to talk about such questions early on. How early may depend on that ticking biological clock, but because you don't want to waste time at any age, and if having children is important to you, jumping on an opportunity to raise this subject could take place any time. By "opportunity" I mean a chance or planned event that naturally triggers the conversation. You're sitting together on a park bench and spot a cute toddler walking around. I see nothing wrong in saying something like "I hope my children are as cute as that." If your date doesn't want to ever have children, you would hope that he or she would speak up at that point. Then you'd have a decision to make about continuing to date this person. If this happened on the first date, then it would be a good thing to have learned that this person doesn't share one of your important goals before proceeding with the relationship. If the relationship is progressing to where it's getting serious, then don't delay in creating an opportunity to discuss this important topic if one doesn't occur spontaneously.

If someone you're dating says words to the effect of "I never want to get married" or "I never want to have children" or "I'm a private person and never want to share my space," thus shooting down one or more of your important goals, I don't see the point of continuing the relationship. Might this person have just been making an immature statement that would change with time? Possibly, but why take the chance? You'd be gambling with your most important asset, your time here on earth.

This example reinforces the point of having goals to begin with. Without goals, you're likely to flounder around the dating scene. If you want your dating life to be successful, you need to be in control of it. Without the road map provided by a set of goals, that will never happen.

Dr. Ruth Westheimer ✅
@AskDrRuth

Dating isn't the goal; rather, dating meets your goals.

Let me end this chapter by inserting a word that I'll bring up again from time to time, which is passion. Finding passion is what many people seek while dating, and that goal is wonderful. But rather than just hoping for passion to find you, I suggest inserting as much passion into your search for Mr. or Ms. Right as you can. The more passionate you are about a task, the more likely you'll succeed. If you look at this search as a chore, it will be. If you look at the glass as half-empty, then it will be. This type of attitude is going to make attaining your goal that much more difficult.

Finding someone who completes you and who fills every day with love and companionship is an incredible blessing. And maybe this search shouldn't be easy, because most things in life that are worth having tend to require some effort. When you make your list of goals, make sure that you include what will be required to keep your attitude toward this process a passionate one.

2.

It Takes Two . . . and Tinder:
How to Meet Someone

Nobody's going to argue with the statement that dating has changed, least of all me. As I've previously said, dating *also* hasn't changed: it is still about meeting that special someone who you hope will one day be magically transformed from "date" to "spouse," or at least "significant other."

That's not to say that there aren't other reasons to date. People often date to avoid being alone. Many activities—from going to a restaurant to seeing a play or movie to watching a gorgeous sunset—are more enjoyable when shared than when done alone. You don't need to see a movie or dine out only on a date. Other people such as roommates, coworkers, fellow students, club members, and friends can share an activity with you. Although it's true you're not alone when you're with one or more people from one of these groups, you're also not on a date.

<u>Stop and Consider:</u> What do you believe makes a date a date?

One answer to this question is that at least for the duration of a date, you're a couple. Yes, you can double date or triple date or gang date, but within these groupings are couples on a date. Dating is different than just being two people sharing an activity together. That difference is the potential for the relationship developing into something more than just friendship.

That potential adds tension. When you're with your best friends, there should be little or no tension. You can make a social gaffe, because if you spill your drink on yourself, all it means is that you'll be the butt of some jokes for the rest of the evening. But when you're on a date, you want everything to go perfectly. You're trying to be more than just yourself. You're a little anxious, and your palms may be a little sweaty. You're thinking about what might happen a bit later in the evening.

Furthermore, dates have a more physical component. I'm not talking about what might take place in bed later on. Rather, while you're together you're likely to come into physical contact, be it a light touch or a body-encircling grasp. And before these touches occur, you're going to anticipate them, wondering if they will happen and at what point on your date. They're the "Will he or she let me?" moments that hang over you as you walk down the street together during the early phase of dating.

An app can never duplicate the various factors that lead up to this tension, because it requires being together in person. Sure, he looks dreamy online and you hope he'll give you a thumbs-up, but if he doesn't, you're really not all that committed, and you're on to the next one in a swipe, soon forgetting all about the first one.

Being able to move on could be an advantage. One of the dangers of the more traditional, face-to-face ways of meeting potential heartthrobs is that you might find yourself in an unrequited love situation. For example, there's that coworker who makes your heart flutter. Although she smiles sweetly when you ask her out, she always has a ready excuse as to why she can't. The problem is that you see her ten times a day, which makes fantasizing about her that much more painful. But the challenge with fantasizing about someone who is unavailable is that those fantasies are tying up your emotions so that you're not available for someone else.

You can also become emotionally tied to someone you meet online. If the two of you don't have regular face-to-face interactions, you can easily force yourself to forget about this person after you realize that the attraction isn't mutual. But if you're seeing this person in class, at work, in the elevator, again and again, then you can fall into this sort of trap, so that every time you see them your heart goes pitter-patter and you are no longer interested in anyone else.

Dr. Ruth Westheimer ✔
@AskDrRuth

Don't allow your emotions to get ahead of reality.

When you're in dating mode, you have to learn to put on the brakes. You can't allow yourself to fall in love with someone who has shown no potential in reciprocating such emotions. And don't say that such emotions are beyond your control. I accept that initially you can feel a strong attraction to someone, but for those feelings to grow into a crush requires that you give in to them. If you allow yourself to constantly daydream about someone who hasn't given any indication that he or she might have an interest in you, or if you fantasize every night about running through a field of daisies together or an even hotter experience, then you're setting yourself up for emotional distress.

You also need to consider how seeing your emotions will affect the other person. If you're both ready for the relationship to blossom, then being openly interested with the other person could be perfect. But you can scare someone away by acting besotted. Hence, remain cool so that the relationship can develop at its own pace.

Romantic emotions aren't under your full control, but they don't have superhuman powers that can overwhelm you . . . unless you let them. Allow such feelings free rein inside your mind, and they'll grow stronger and stronger until it will take quite an effort to curtail the effect that they're having. Better to push thoughts that are premature out of your mind, so that you're not setting yourself up for a fall.

The technique that I recommend to accomplish this is a bit like Woody Allen's comedy routine in which he explains that he thinks about baseball while making love to keep himself from ejaculating too quickly. If you find yourself drifting into fantasies with someone you barely know but want to know better, divert those thoughts by thinking of something else entirely. You could concentrate on an upcoming chore or switch the object of your desire and daydream about an unavailable movie star you find attractive. The trick is to fill the void in your head so that you don't have any room for thoughts about this person who, as far as you know, isn't into you the way you are into him or her—at least not yet. If a spark develops at some point in the future, great, but until that happens, keep these emotions locked down.

Depending on your personality, this may take some effort, especially if you have a history of falling in love with people who don't love you back. If you've followed that pattern, you've trained your brain to work against you. Gaining the needed discipline won't be that easy. You might need some time to develop control, but you can do it. The effects of diverting thoughts about this person may not be apparent right away, but over time you'll see that the hold he or she has on your romantic soul will weaken, and it will become easier and easier to control your feelings.

Although this chapter is about how to meet that person in the first place, here I am telling you how to forget about someone you haven't even dated yet. I have good reason: some of you start to daydream about someone you've met online but not yet in person, which is a huge mistake, because if you do finally meet, your expectations might be unrealistic. Even if your date is quite suitable, if you've put this person on a pedestal, you're going to be disappointed. As a result, prepare yourself for the dating experience by making sure that you keep both feet on the ground at all times.

Not bringing enthusiasm to your search for a date won't work either. If flipping through hundreds of pictures has become boring, or if you tell yourself that you can't read one more profile that sounds like every other one, then that's going to be a huge hindrance. The sweet spot is somewhere between falling head over heels in love with someone you've never met and never bothering to look at profiles because their pictures leave you cold.

According to some statistics I've seen, more than 70 percent of singles meet other singles through e-dating. Considering that not all that long ago this method of dating didn't even exist, that number reflects tremendous change. And it must be a change for the better, because these methods have been around long enough that if the majority of their users weren't successful, people would have stopped employing them by now. Clearly online dating is more than just a fad. It's now the main way that single adults meet each other. Notice I said "adults." Young people who are still in school, whether that be high school or college, may glance at apps like Tinder for entertainment purposes, but because they're surrounded by other single people their own age, they tend not to actually use such apps to date. Instead, they select dating partners from among their schoolmates or they go out in groups rather than dating. Thus, the traditional methods of dating continue among the young, but if they don't lead to a committed relationship by graduation, you can be sure that a switch to using tech for dating will occur soon after, if not before then.

What if you find yourself single in your forties, fifties, or older? You may be somewhat tech savvy, but you might tell yourself that you'll never be able to find dates using your phone. Let me say two things. First, you have experience using the old tried-and-true methods, so you should certainly turn to them. (I discuss this topic more elsewhere in the chapter.) Second, using an app isn't that difficult. If you use one that asks you to sign in with Facebook, you'll immediately see that the app knows a lot about you, certainly your age, so you'll be presented with people in your age group. Many of those people will be in the same boat: a little gun-shy about using an app to date. And even if they've become accustomed to using apps, they'll remember what it was like when they first started down this path, so they'll be sympathetic. Don't tell yourself that you're too old to enter this new dating age, but instead force yourself to jump right in.

Many individuals over forty complain that these apps have made the dating process feel shallow. You've gathered a lot of experience in your life, and suddenly all that seems to matter is what you look like in a picture. If you've gathered some physical signs of aging, you might not be enchanted by what you see in your picture. Keep in mind that every other single person your age is in a similar situation. If you consider some of the things you can do on your phone or computer today and think about how technology has made it easier to search for knowledge, shop, or find your way, then you can have faith that dating in today's world will also be easier after you figure out the ropes of using technology.

Keeping up with all the various e-dating methods is nearly impossible, but as I write this book I've found more than thirty, including Adult FriendFinder, BlackPeopleMeet, Blue, Bumble, ChristianMingle, Clover, Coffee Meets Bagel, eHarmony, EliteSingles, First, Grindr, happn, Hinge, How About We, It's Just Lunch, JDate, Loveflutter, Match, OkCupid, OurTime, PlentyOfFish, ProfessionalMatch, SCRUFF, SeniorPeopleMeet, ShowReal, SingleParentMeet, Tawkify Tender, Tinder, Willow, Wingman, and Zoosk. By the time this book is published, some of these apps will have disappeared and new ones will be gaining traction, so instead of writing about each one of them, I'm going to stick to general advice. If you want more specifics about any of these sites, you can find plenty of material on the internet.

Not all these apps are going to be right for you. Whether you want to use an app that caters to a specific niche you're in, or if you prefer an app with a broader market, is something you can decide after some experimentation. Given the many options, you need to do some research before you begin your quest.

But to tell you the truth, I don't suggest picking one of these services based only on online reviews. Wait to make your choice until after you've surveyed your friends and relatives who've used an app and who live near you. I have a number of reasons for saying so. First, even though these dating services are national in scope, the number of singles in a given area is variable. Finding a site with eligible people who all live five hundred or more miles away from you isn't going to be fruitful when looking for a date for Saturday night. If you live in or near a densely populated city, which all have a large pool of singles, just about any of these dating apps will be able to offer a large selection. But if you don't live in a metropolis, some of these apps and sites don't offer you much of a choice. How do you tell which is the best one for where you're located? As I said, ask around. Information on which dating site has the most singles listed on it in your area is news that's likely to make the rounds with your friends and coworkers. And conversely, if one site seems geographically oriented to where you live, singles in your area will be drawn to it, and therefore, you should be too. Unless you're willing to spend hours joining every app and checking out their listings near you, you can only get the information by asking people who share your locale.

If you live in a rural area, e-dating may not be for you unless you're willing to travel. If only a limited amount of single people in your age bracket live within driving distance, then you might meet them all in a short period of time, and if none are right, you'll be out of luck. Don't let your geography force you into being miserable. If you're willing to travel to nearby communities, then you can search the singles pool in those places.

Another reason to ask around before choosing a dating site is that you can easily find negative reviews of all these apps and sites. The more popular an app or site is, the more negative reviews you can discover. I'm not telling you to ignore them. In fact, I think you should read some of them so that you understand the dangers that lurk out there and can better protect yourself against them.

For example, some of the apps where you swipe through pictures of singles have many bots. Bots aren't real people; some company has set up a fake profile looking to make money off of you rather than help you find a dating partner. If you see a picture of someone who is extremely attractive and with little accompanying bio information, there's a good chance that this profile is a bot and not a real person. Because many of these bots have foreign sources, if anything is written on the page, look for misspellings and grammatical errors, which are sure signs that these "people" don't exist.

The truth is that people are more likely to air their gripes than spend time praising a site. That's just human nature. If you feel you've been wronged, you want revenge, and so you'll shout it from the rooftops—of the internet anyway. However, millions of people have been extremely happy e-dating, so these sites clearly offer a valuable service. You just may have difficulty finding the praise they deserve, because their satisfied customers might not bother writing reviews.

How much value you can get from a site or app may depend on how much you're willing to spend. Many of these dating sites will let you sign up for free, maybe at a certain level or for a trial period, but they won't give you full access to all the features unless you pay a monthly fee to be a member. Because you won't have full access to all they can do, you'll be missing out on much of what they have to offer. There's nothing wrong with making money, and if a site makes you pay, you would expect to get more out of that site. Therefore, be careful about judging a site only by what you can get for free. If you can meet people on one of these sites or apps without paying anything, then good for you. But if you feel as if you're not meeting the right people, even though others have reported that you should be, or the experience isn't enjoyable, then think about paying some money before giving up. These sites and apps couldn't charge additional fees if they weren't offering something of value to their paying customers, so maybe these added services are exactly what you need to help you to find a match. And if one aspect of these added services is better security, which often is part of the paid package, then I'd say paying the monthly fee is well worth the investment. Think about it: trolls who use these sites often don't pay or give real information such as a credit card account number, so the people you meet among the paid users are likely to be more reliable.

Some sites ask you to answer a lot of questions about yourself and the type of person you're looking for, whereas others don't care how much of a profile you include. The sites that have you fill out a long profile are considered more serious, meaning that the people on them often are looking for long-term relationships. Those sites generally charge for their efforts on your behalf and also take much more of a time commitment. Not only do you have to fill out the forms, but you also have to read what those people recommended to you have to say, or else you have to spend time discussing your likes and dislikes with a representative. That's why many people prefer the sites and apps that offer the instant gratification of swiping through pictures of people who are nearby. But these days many people also report that swiping gets old—it's like playing the same video game over and over. If you find that happening to you, then maybe it's time to try a more serious site and/or other methods of finding dates.

I advise that you try both. The process of sites like eHarmony, Match, or It's Just Lunch might be slower, but more of the people on these sites are serious about wanting a relationship rather than a one-night stand. Because people are impatient by nature, a lot of those on the swipe-through-the-pictures sites like Tinder aren't limited just to those looking for sex. So while you're waiting to meet your ideal mate on a "serious" site, going out on some "swipe" dates might keep you from getting impatient and might even land you The One.

A common complaint I read about many of these paid sites is that after you agree to pay to be a member, they make it difficult to end your membership. You can probably end the automatic payments by calling your credit card company, but you might want to be extra careful before signing up and certainly limit yourself to only one or two paid sites.

I also caution you about using your primary e-mail address, especially if you get work e-mails on it. You can easily get a second e-mail address that you can afford to scrap if your inbox is getting filled with unwanted e-mails. (Remember that population of bots.) Before you sign up to one of these sites or apps using your Facebook account, if your Facebook account is an important resource for you, then I suggest you think twice. If your Facebook account gets compromised in some way, you'll regret it. At the very least, make only a minimum of your Facebook page public and keep the rest private, or if a site allows you to sign up using an e-mail address rather than your Facebook account, select that. Another option is to use only dating sites and apps that don't require a Facebook account, such as OkCupid and Willow (an app that doesn't show pictures until later in the process, so it could be considered the anti-Tinder).

The internet is a big place, so bear in mind that you're not limited to dating sites to find fellow singles online. For example, I know a couple who met playing online Scrabble and ended up marrying. If you have some interest that takes you to several sites where you interact with others, don't be afraid to reveal that you're single and looking for a partner, because you never know what might happen. You also haven't wasted any time if you don't find a partner, because that wasn't the main reason you initially visited that site.

<u>Stop and Consider:</u> The information you put on a dating website is bait.

If you're going to look for dates using online dating sites and apps, then I suggest you jump all the way in and not make a halfhearted attempt. If you don't put your best foot forward, then you're more likely to attract people who you don't find worthy of a relationship, assuming you attract anybody at all. I understand the temptation of saying to yourself, *Oh well, this probably isn't going to work, but let me just see what happens.* You're giving yourself an excuse so that if it doesn't work for you, you can say that you didn't really try. In that scenario you're setting yourself up for failure. Instead make sure that the information you provide, including any visuals, is of the highest quality and shows you in your best light. Let others—friends, coworkers, siblings—look at what you write for your profile and offer suggestions to improve it before you post it. Consider having professional photographs taken or give the ones you do have to a friend who's an expert at Photoshop to make them pop. Give yourself every chance at success instead of only a small chance. If no one bites, so be it, but at least you gave it your all.

No matter what, don't lie. By "lie" I mean posting pictures of yourself that are five years old or only show your face because you need to lose a few pounds, or mentioning you went to college when you didn't. Lies may get you some initial dates, but when those lies are exposed, your date will be disappointed in the real you, and he or she is going to run the other way. Being truthful may cost you some dates, but if you rack up a long string of one-time dates because of lying, then you're not going to feel any better about yourself.

Let me further address this need to lie. One common problem women face is that the world, as represented by what the media depicts, expects everyone to be skinny, and yet most of the population isn't. But being overweight comes with more baggage than just the extra pounds.

If you're overweight, you may be thought of as lazy or as someone who doesn't care about your appearance. In this instance, in order to let those individuals who look at your pictures know how much you do care about your health and appearance, train for some short race, like a 5K, and then post a picture of yourself when you reached the finish line. Yes, people who look at your photographs are going to know that you're overweight, but they'll also get the message that you're healthy and active. This is one of those pictures that tells a thousand words. Yes, you might scare away some couch potatoes, but maybe that's a good thing!

You don't have a college degree? Take a picture of yourself playing chess or sitting with a book in a library. Think your nose is too big? Post a picture of yourself singing karaoke; it will show you're fun loving and the mic will balance your nose. Remember, this isn't your high school yearbook where the same photographer takes a similar picture of every student. Use your imagination to figure out ways to show yourself off in these pictures. The more you hate yourself in pictures the more creative you'll have to be, but trust me that you can produce pictures that add to your appeal rather than detract from it. The key is to be proactive rather than trying to post a "fake" you.

If you can't figure out a pose or two to put your best foot forward, ask around. You probably know a few people who are into photography. Ask them to help you and see what advice they have.

Some of you without dates feel that even the need to find a date is embarrassing, so you don't want to ask for help. If you're sick, you go to a doctor, and if your car breaks down, you take it to a mechanic, so don't be afraid of asking for help to find yourself some dates. There's no shame in wanting to date; everybody does it, so don't put your head in the sand.

<u>Stop and Consider:</u> Are you ashamed of needing someone to date?

By the way, I know some absolutely gorgeous models who have problems with dating. Some men are afraid to ask them out, others only want to be able to say they took them to bed, whereas still others are looking for arm candy rather than a lover and best friend. So whatever issues you have with dating, stop obsessing over them, and do whatever it takes to overcome them.

These apps can be important to those individuals who move to a new place. If you're new in town, then you don't have a social circle to fall back on. By getting dates on an app, even if the people you date turn out not to be your next full-time partner, they might end up as friends that could be building blocks to a new social life.

Another group of people who use these apps have a home base but travel a lot for work. Many of them are just looking for a night of sex while on the road and even may be married. Having a one-night stand is a strong temptation, I understand, but cheating on a spouse often leads to the breakup of a marriage, so if you don't want to be involved and if you suspect someone asking you for a date is cheating, then pass.

Dr. Ruth Westheimer ✓
@AskDrRuth

Humor on a dating app can be a positive and a negative.

Making people laugh is integral to social interactions. The guy at the party who is good at telling jokes will probably draw a crowd, unless they're all offensive jokes. And saying you like to travel and go to the movies when writing your profile on an app isn't going to make you stand out from the crowd. Humor can increase your chances of a right, rather than left, swipe, but the wrong type of humor can make those swipes go the other way.

Some types of humor are less appreciated than others, and if you tell jokes that aren't in good taste, you risk turning some people off.

On the other hand, you should get some points for trying. Many men complain that women on these apps take their attempts at humor too seriously, overanalyzing them rather than just accepting a joke for what it is: a joke. When men are together, they're always trying to top each other with the best joke, and many think this is also the way to a woman's heart. But not every attempt at humor is going to be appreciated by women, so I advise men to use humor carefully, and I advise women not to take humor in a profile too seriously.

Dr. Ruth Westheimer ✓
@AskDrRuth

Treat humor like a spice.

If you use too much salt or pepper, you can easily ruin a good meal. The same goes for humor and your profile. Treat humor like a spice in cooking. It can enhance your profile, but if you pour it on with a heavy hand, it will completely mask the flavor of the main dish. Sprinkle a little humor on your profile but not too much. Also, if your profile is on the light side when it comes to accomplishments, then I advise using humor judiciously, because humor will only further lighten your image and might make you seem too weightless to bother with. On the other hand, if you're one of those people with a ton of degrees and a fancy job, you might want to use some humor to show that you're not a boring workaholic that someone looking for a good time should steer away from.

I haven't addressed one danger with dating sites and apps that can occur when people prefer to stay home flipping through various dating sites without any intention of ever going on a date. You could call it a dating substitute. Friends may do this together by looking at the various pictures that people post and making fun of them.

Many people much younger than me seem to live on their phones, which become an appendage rather than a tool. But what studies have shown is that spending so much time on a phone ends up making these young people depressed. We humans need physical human contact. The purpose of dating is to bring one human being together with another. Having people come together as couples is important not only for continuing our species but also for supporting the mental health of every individual.

Although these dating sites can be a form of entertainment, much as sitting at a café in Paris and commenting on the people walking by was when I was a student there, don't use these apps as a substitute for actual physical social contact. I don't care whether you meet other people on an app or any other way, don't lock yourself in a room pretending you're dating when you're not even really making an attempt to find a date.

For those of you who are meeting success using one or more of these sites or apps, at least to the extent that you're getting dates even if you haven't found the perfect partner yet, then stick with this method. However, if you're not satisfied, then also give the more traditional methods of finding a partner a try. The following is some advice on which ones might work for you and how to maximize their effectiveness.

One method for finding dates that I favor is to tell everyone you know that you're looking. And when I say *everyone*, I mean everyone, not just your close friends. Even someone who seems unlikely—your grandmother, for example—might know someone else who knows of a single person your age. (Even if she lives in a facility for the elderly, the residents always get together to talk at mealtimes and during activities, and your grandmother is going to spread the word because she'd be proud if she found someone for you.) If you have a whole army of people on the lookout, the odds of success increase.

These requests can be both general and specific. A general request, "I'm single and I need to find a partner," is more likely to be forgotten or put on the back burner. I'm not saying not to ask for help this way, but understand that the more specific you are, the more likely people will be to act. Even when people really want to help you, if they're busy, they might put off playing matchmaker and eventually even forget the request. Telling a varied group of people that you scored tickets to such-and-such an event a month from now and that you need a date—making it clear that there's a time limit—might get them to put more energy into their search on your behalf. If you can't find a date, then you can go to the event with a friend, so the ticket won't really go to waste, but why not use an excuse like this to light a fire under those you've asked to help?

By the way, putting some of your hard-earned cash on the line will help you on this search as well. Doing something like buying tickets to a concert ahead of time will spur you to do whatever you can to find a date. You might not think you need such an incentive, but there's a good chance that you do.

I haven't mentioned speed dating yet. You might think that because I put so much value in saving time, I'd be a big fan of it, but I'm not. If you had an invitation to a wedding and needed some arm candy of either the male or female variety, then perhaps speed dating would be an appropriate way to acquire a date for this one occasion, but when finding romance, the pressure-cooker atmosphere of speed dating is probably just going to melt any romance away.

Many people who attend these speed-dating events do it for the entertainment value, as if they were going bowling, and I have no problem with that. However, the few minutes you're together with your fellow speed daters means that the chief factor in deciding whether to select someone will be appearance, so the main descriptive word to apply to these dates is shallow—and that approach is unlikely to help you meet your goal of finding your one true love. If one of your goals is to allocate five hours a week to finding a partner, don't count the time spent speed dating as applicable.

For those of you who believe that before these dating sites came into existence, people were on their own when it came to finding a mate, your conclusion is off by thousands of years. You can find matchmakers mentioned in the Bible, and be sure that every culture has had someone serving this task. After humans put two and two together and realized that sex led to babies, and therefore heirs, matchmakers popped up everywhere. It's simply the law of supply and demand: people have always sought spouses; whether it was the person getting married or the parents, there have always been people ready to take money to help. And the better the matches that were made, the more this person could charge.

In big cities, professional matchmakers, whether individuals or small companies, still exist. Some are aimed at pairing those individuals with fat wallets and so can charge a lot of money, up to half a million dollars, while others cost less, though no professional matchmakers come cheap. These matchmakers offer individualized service, so you're not dealing with a large impersonal company but instead receiving one-on-one service that can include everything from making initial matches to arranging every aspect of each date.

Take some comfort in knowing the long history of the art of matchmaking, because it shows that you're far from alone in having problems finding dates, though until recently matchmakers only tried to make permanent matches, not one-night stands. I've played matchmaker a few times, not for money, but because in the Jewish tradition, making a match is a mitzvah, a blessing that can help one get into heaven, and you can never have too many Get Out of Jail Free cards, can you?

Why spend more money on a matchmaker when some dating apps or sites are free or at least less costly? The answer is personal service. If you feel you need more help than just being presented with potential dates, then a matchmaker might be right for you. After you become a client of a matchmaker, he or she will intercede on your behalf, acting as your agent to try to convince others that you're worth pursuing. The fees don't guarantee a lifetime partner, but there's an implied guarantee that you'll get a lot of hand-holding, and some people, especially those who've had little success from dating online, can benefit greatly from that. Because most matchmakers focus on a specific geographic area, you won't have to worry about being paired with someone who lives hundreds of miles away.

Stop and Consider: Does having some skin in the game, i.e. some money invested, serve to motivate you?

Are you someone who complains about being single? Perhaps what you need is some more motivation in order to get your dating house in order. Complaining and procrastinating are easy, but they won't lead to finding a date. Some people are easily self-motivated, while others need a parent/teacher/boss/drill sergeant to get them to take action. The more of a dillydallier you are, the more you need to find ways to motivate yourself.

And this may be even truer in the age of swiping. Swiping the screen takes almost no effort, and if you believe swiping is all it takes to find a date, then your subconscious may tell you that you don't need to bother to do anything more. That's an acceptable attitude if you're getting dates, but if you're not, or if you're not getting the right kind of dates, then you need to do more than just swipe. If you're the type of person who continually procrastinates, then in order to meet any success in the dating game, you need to find ways to motivate yourself.

Today most people seem to be busier than people were in the past, and these apps are efficient in that you don't have to waste time hanging out someplace hoping to meet someone, but rather you can spend a little time with an app and probably set up a date. But if all the dates you arrange are one-time only, then you're not really being all that efficient, are you? You might have to be a little harsh on yourself, but look back at your recent dating history. If it's not satisfactory, then give other methods a try.

What if you're not that busy, maybe because you're out of a job, and so you're also not that flush when it comes to finding the cash for dating? Does that mean that you're not able to date? Although money is an important factor when it comes to dating, so is time. If you have additional free time because you're unemployed, then use it to your best advantage. You can spend more time swiping than people who are working full-time, and you might be able to use an app like this as part of your job search. If you come across as sincere in wanting to find both a partner and a job, who knows, you might get lucky in hitting both lotteries.

Another way of meeting people is to hang out with the in-crowd, those individuals who are always throwing parties and events where lots of single people mingle. You're not a member of the in-crowd, you say? Maybe not today, but that doesn't mean you can't be in the near future. The in-crowd is not a closed club. You probably know at least one or two people who always seem to be going to this or that party or event, so make friends with them. Do them a favor at the first possible opportunity. Get yourself invited to one party, and then make friends so that you're invited to other events. What do I mean by "make friends"? For example, don't arrive empty-handed, but instead bring a six-pack of beer or a bottle of wine or a dozen doughnuts. Instead of being the last one there, after everyone has already broken up into little groups, be one of the first there. When other single people arrive, waiting for their friends, you can talk to them; hopefully they'll introduce you to their friends. If you're talking to one person and you see someone else standing by him or herself, ask that person over and introduce everyone. If the host needs help setting up, volunteer. You don't have to stand out as the most liked individual; you just have to contribute enough to the group that when invitations are sent out for the next event, you get one.

Some of you were never able to break into this social circle when you were in high school and so have decided that those people aren't for you. Although that reaction is understandable, it's a mistake. You're no longer a teenager, and the adults I'm urging you to befriend aren't either. Adults judge people differently. They're less cliquish because they've matured and understand better how to appreciate others. Not every adult is this way, but most are. If you can bring something to the table, then you'll be accepted. Figure out what you have to offer and then go out and sell it. You may be good at telling jokes, or perhaps your computer skills would be useful in keeping the party invitation list updated. Just figure out what you have to offer and try to insinuate yourself into some social group. You might feel a bit awkward at first. You might get rejected, but sitting home alone isn't exactly a bowl of cherries either. By taking action, you'll feel better about yourself and your dating situation.

As I said earlier, I also tell people to partake in activities they enjoy not just online but in the real world, where they might meet a single person. For example, if you like foreign films, take a class at a community college on that subject. At least you'll see some films even if you don't end up with a moviegoing partner. If you take a cooking class you'll learn to prepare delicious meals, or if it's a baking class you'll get to sample some delicious treats, so it will be time well spent regardless of whether you find someone to share your kitchen. If you have a camera that sits unused because you don't really understand all the buttons, you might find a new lifetime hobby if not a new lifetime model by taking a photography class. There's nothing wrong with trying your hand at something new. If you've always admired pottery, why not take a class on how to use a potter's wheel and make your own bowls? Even if you decide it's not for you, you've learned something valuable.

While taking one of these classes, you might meet another single person, but if you don't, at least you'll have learned some more about a subject that interests you. When at some other point you do meet someone, you'll have something new to talk about. Lots of opportunities like this are available, especially if you live in a city. Many colleges have an adult education department, and they know that single people use these courses as a means of meeting people.

Other options are available if you don't want to take a class. You can join a hiking or sailing club. You can volunteer at a wide range of nonprofit organizations, such as an animal shelter. Or you could be a museum docent, for example. Depending on the organization, you might meet older adults, but there'll be some young people as well. Don't forget, anyone you meet who takes a shine to you might be the source of meeting that special single person, as long as you reveal that you're looking.

>  **Dr. Ruth Westheimer** ✓
> @AskDrRuth
>
> Don't be vain and pretend that your social calendar is full when it isn't.

In today's society not having an active social life can be embarrassing, but if you pretend that you do when you don't, you could be missing the opportunity to meet people who could fill your social calendar. Hence, be open about being single, and the more likely—and quickly—you won't be single.

Is it better to take part in an activity like some of those I've just mentioned alone or with a friend? The friend will provide companionship, but the friend also makes you somewhat unavailable when meeting other people in the class or activity. The answer to this question depends on who the friend is and how well you work together. If you suddenly cross the room to go talk to some single person you spot and this friend won't mind, then having this friend along might be all right. But if you'll feel the least bit inhibited by having this friend there and feel badly for abandoning him or her, or if this friend is a competitor on the dating scene, then go alone. True, if you've chosen wisely it's an activity that you'll enjoy even if you don't meet any potential dates, but part of your incentive is to meet someone.

Doing something that you're passionate about is an excellent way to meet others who share that passion. Don't worry about their ages or whether they're single or part of a couple; just do all you can to make this group of friends who share your passion as large as possible. All these people will think favorably about you because you share the same passion, and so they'll introduce you to other connections, and this network will help you to find dates. Being passionate about something makes your personality shine, which can leave a good impression on people around you who will actively want to help you find a significant other.

What if you're not passionate about anything? Let's put aside dating for a moment. Having activities, hobbies, and interests that arouse passionate feelings in you are part of what makes life worthwhile. And the more you are enjoying life, the more others will be attracted to you. I suggest looking for an outside interest that makes you excited, whether it actually leads you to meet anyone to date or not.

And if your passion is a solitary activity, like reading mysteries, maybe you should set it aside for a while and try to expand your horizons. You could do that within the scope of your favorite activity by volunteering at a library or joining a book club. Perhaps you could choose an activity that's entirely unrelated. Humans need other humans, so adding to your list of what you like to do a few interests that bring you in contact with others will benefit you in many ways. Might it also help you find a partner? Of course, but even more important is how it can benefit you as an individual.

Dr. Ruth Westheimer ✓
@AskDrRuth

Escapism is okay from time to time, but you don't want to escape from humanity altogether.

Many people hate the bar scene, but you can meet singles in other places. Your local laundromat is one, especially if you live in a neighborhood populated by singles. If a food co-op is near you, join and you never know whom you'll meet while stocking the shelves. If you have a dog, walking it around your neighborhood will serve to introduce you to all the other dog owners. If there's a block association, join it, and if there isn't one, start one. Soon everyone on your block will know who you are. Investigate the nearby clubs that support whatever political party you belong to or cause you support. If you take public transportation, get your eyes out of your book or off your screen while traveling and look around. You might meet a sympathetic gaze in return, and a simple wink might serve as an introduction!

If you belong to a religion, even if you don't practice regularly, functions held at places of worship are often a good source of meeting people. Some religious organizations actually try to help singles find each other by holding functions aimed at attracting singles. And notice I said religious institutions are a good place for meeting people—not just single people. Yes, single might be preferable because you're on the prowl, but remember what I said about telling everyone that you're looking. By broadening the number of people you know, you'll also be widening the net you're casting.

Although the bar and club scene does have negative aspects, it also has some positive ones—primarily that a lot of people in a bar or club are on the lookout for a partner. Granted, many may be seeking someone for only that evening, but some are also looking for long-term romance. How can I be so confident in that statement? Because if millions of people are looking for love on the various apps and dating sites, then some of them are bound to show up at a bar or club where singles gather also.

If you go to one of these places with some friends, you'll have a good time whether or not you meet someone. And, yes, some of you will be approached by people trying to impress you, while others of you will have to gather up your courage to talk to someone and maybe spend some money buying drinks. If you keep it light, not turning anyone down in a mean way and not getting angry if someone won't talk to you, then the experience won't be bad. Plenty of relationships have started in these environments, so going isn't a lost cause by any means.

Of course, not every bar attracts singles. Some are hangouts for older men who just need a place to get away and be with their friends. As a result, check out your local bar scene online and locate the ones that cater to your type of singles crowd, the chief selection factor being age. I'm not encouraging you to just go out drinking; I want to help you meet the love of your life.

What if no matter what you try, you can't seem to land a date and you just can't figure out why? Or you get first dates but not second ones. What if the years are ticking away, and you're batting average is stuck in the low numbers? One common reason may be shyness, especially among men who traditionally are supposed to do the asking, though these days with apps like Tinder, things are changing. Fear paralyzes some people, both men and women, and the older they get, the more that fear plays a part in not being able to find anyone. What kinds of fear? For men it might be a fear of looking foolish in bed because they've had so little practice or have a small penis, whether or not their penis really is that small. For women it can be a body image issue or, if they're a virgin, being afraid that their first time will be painful. For both sexes the fear can simply be the fear of rejection. If you barely put yourself out there, or not at all, then you can't be rejected.

The heterosexual dating scene has posed one particular difficulty for men: Because they're the ones who are traditionally supposed to make the first move, they run the risk of being rejected, potentially over and over again. Some women have always known how to signal their interest, such as the women in olden times who would drop their handkerchief within the line of sight of a man who interested them. If he came over and picked it up, their courtship might proceed. The women who employed such tactics were willing to take the risk that the man might simply leave that handkerchief where it fell. With online dating, both sexes now have the opportunity to be rejected, because they can swipe their interest in the photo of someone on a dating site and not get the return message they seek, though it seems from my research that men seeking women remain more likely to get rejected. On the other hand, not being given a positive swipe back won't cause quite the embarrassment that being turned down in person does. In addition, because being turned down happens quite often on these dating apps, it also means rejection loses some of its sting—but not all of it, and certainly not if all someone is getting is rejection.

Dr. Ruth Westheimer ✓
@AskDrRuth

Take inspiration from the turtle.

I have a collection of turtles—not real ones, just little artificial turtles in stone or metal. (The number of such turtles I've bought is small, but my collection is rather large because people keep giving them to me.) I admire turtles because in order to get anywhere they have to stick their neck out. In their shell they are safe, but to get food and find a mate, they have to move around. To me the turtle is a symbol of what it means to be brave, which is why I like to surround myself with them in my apartment.

I admit rejection is hard and an emotion you'd prefer to avoid. But if you're going to succeed in life, it's unavoidable, so you might as well get over this fear of being rejected and join everyone else looking for dates. If you don't, you'll never find true love, and that would be a much worse fate than being rejected from time to time.

Of course, you can't allow yourself to become completely inured to rejection. As I've been saying, online dating speeds up the initial contacts between people to almost lightning speed. If you start to expect rejection because you've been rejected so many times, you may then lose the incentive to change, blaming the online dating system entirely for what has been happening. Yes, you probably face more rejection when you use an online dating service, but you might also be somewhat at fault, so you have to look in the mirror to see whether you can change in ways that will reduce the rejections you receive, or more importantly, land you that one key acceptance that you've been waiting for.

Stop and Consider: Are you wandering around lost in a dating desert?

Because there are several potential sources for your lack of success at dating, figuring out the cause of being stuck in a dating desert is the first priority. If you can do something about it, then you have to make whatever changes are necessary. But often it's not as simple as going out and buying a new wardrobe. If you're suffering from a lack of self-confidence, for example, then self-confidence is something you can't order for yourself on Amazon. (By the way, overconfidence can also be a turnoff, so if you tend to brag a lot on a first date and never get second dates, try keeping the boasts to a minimum.)

Going to see a professional counselor would probably be a good idea if you're really miserable and can't see a way out of your situation. Maybe you're missing something obvious or just need someone to help motivate you, but I understand that finding and affording a counselor can be difficult.

If you have the impression that you're not datable, one suggestion I can make that won't cost anything is to ask your friends for help. See if one or two will mentor you. You can take them into your confidence, show them what's on your profile, and tell them what you're doing to get dates. A good mentor will be critical, so don't expect to get only pats on the back for trying. If your mentor feels that you're doing something wrong, you need to listen to what he or she has to say. If you're going to be defensive and make an excuse for every criticism, then you may as well not bother seeking out a mentor.

One powerful inducement a mentor gives you is that now you have someone looking over your shoulder. If you don't have a date for the coming weekend, your mentor is going to ask you what you're doing about it. Often making excuses to yourself is easier than making them to someone else, so hopefully your mentor will goad you into action.

Your mentor and other friends can also help you by accompanying you on your search for people to date. If you go with them to a place where other singles your age gather, you'll have a chance to mingle without feeling alone and a complete outsider. You can get used to talking and interacting with prospective dates. Show the world that you're an active, social individual, and don't be overly picky. I'm sure you're going to meet some other lonely single people, so just make sure that you go out on some dates as a result of this mixing. Be a little aggressive. After you enter the world of dating, the process of asking someone for a date and going on dates will become easier. But if you sit at home waiting for a miracle, then more than likely you're not going to meet with much success.

And don't be the first one to go home, even if you're a little discouraged. As the night goes on, the single people who don't land their dream date will start to look further afield. I know that it's unfair that ten eligible people don't surround you the minute you walk through the door, but you have to learn to play the hand you're dealt.

Dr. Ruth Westheimer ✔
@AskDrRuth

If your biological clock is ticking, be extra careful about who you date.

If you're a woman of a certain age still single and childless, then you may have heard your biological clock ticking, and if you want to have children, you can't waste much more time. I don't want to use the word *desperate*, but you may feel pressured because of that ticking clock. The problem is that any feelings of desperation also make you more vulnerable. Unfortunately some guys out there prey on women in this situation. They've understood that women who face this situation will be more willing to have sex with a man who has the potential to be the father of their children in order to hold onto him. The problem is that after they have sex, he's going to cut and run because the last thing he wants is to father children.

Being able to read the mind of someone you meet online and have dated once or twice is difficult. As long as you enjoyed a sexual encounter, in general there's no harm done just because you had sex after a date or two with a partner whom, when you were younger, you might have waited longer to have sex with. But a woman who's feeling the pressure of finding a mate might say yes to having sex when she really isn't ready.

There's no clear-cut solution to this situation other than to not let the signals your "danger" antenna are sending get drowned out by the ticking of that biological clock.

I wish that I didn't have to add anything on a subject as terrible as rape, but everyone knows that some men out there try to take advantage of women, so I can't ignore the topic. I've been telling you to be safe, but I want to add that I don't believe that women should rely only on these new rules of consent that are being promulgated to keep themselves safe. In an ideal world, it would be wonderful if everyone could communicate their wishes regarding each level of sexual contact and not be pushed to go any further, but we don't live in such a world. Therefore, women need to be as cautious as possible when on a date with someone who isn't a romantic partner they already trust.

I'm a New Yorker, and like many of my fellow New Yorkers, I didn't always wait for the light to turn green to cross the street. But then a couple of my friends got hurt, and now, as impatient a person as I am, I never attempt to cross when the sign says "Don't Walk." That doesn't mean some car or bicycle that's turning or goes through a red light couldn't hit me, but I'm using common sense to limit the risks I take. Dating always will have some inherent risks, but you can lower the odds of finding yourself in a dangerous situation by using common sense and erring on the side of caution.

3.

Mentally and Physically Preparing for That First Date

There are two types of first dates. In the first type, you know the person. Maybe you don't know the person well, but if it's someone who's been part of your social life at school or work, or you spent some time together talking in a bar, then you two are at least vaguely familiar with each other, if only on a surface level. The second type of first date includes dates you've arranged on an online dating site or app and those others have arranged, such as blind dates; in both cases, your dates are people you've never met. You'd think you would know a lot more about a social media date than a blind date others have arranged for you, because you've been communicating for a certain amount of time and exchanged at least some basic information. Where a blind date is more of a blank slate, a first date with someone you met online brings with it expectations, which can be more challenging to having a successful first date than knowing little about the person. Most people will have the tendency to paint themselves in the best possible light, which makes it far more likely that based on what you think you know about this person, you're more likely to be disappointed than pleasantly surprised. As a result, learning to discount expectations is an important lesson of first dates with someone you met online.

I suggest that you spend as little time as possible thinking about this person until you actually meet. If you allow your imagination to roam free, you'll tend to build up your expectations, and why wouldn't you, as you certainly want any date to yield the next love of your life? Because reining in your imagination on the subject of what this person you're going to meet will be like is difficult, focus on keeping your imagination from infiltrating your brain altogether.

This process of meeting someone you only know from online dating is somewhat like shopping for clothes online. You see a picture, but until UPS delivers the garment to your door, you try it on, and look in the mirror, you can't tell whether or not it really looks good on you. Your mother buying you something to wear is more like a blind date. She knows your tastes and what you look like, but she still might choose a top for you that you instantly conclude looks atrocious. Sometimes she gets it right and you love it, and it's the same with first dates. Some are awful and some deliver into your lap the love of your life.

Dr. Ruth Westheimer ●
@AskDrRuth

Dr. Ruth Tweets: Your attitude on a date is extremely important.

Your attitude about dating is going to have an effect on your dating experience. If your approach to dating is to take it too seriously, if you're too nervous before a date, or if you're miserable when you walk out the door to go to meet someone new, then it's more than likely that your dates won't be all that much fun. Yes, you have an important goal—to find a loving partner—but that goal doesn't mean that you can't enjoy the process.

People are fascinating. Even the boring ones have something to offer if you dig a little. But you have to bring the right attitude to a date in order to get the most from it. You have to say to yourself, *I'm going to enjoy this date. I'm going to try to be my funniest. I'm going to tell some of my best stories and hope this person is going to offer something of equal value.* Say to yourself, *Even if very early in the evening we both know that this date is never going to be repeated, we can still both have a good time.*

Don't allow your expectations to soar ahead of time. At the same time keep a positive attitude. Whatever your trepidations about this date, don't allow them to spin things worse than they're likely to be, even if your aunt that you don't like set up the blind date. By remaining positive you're more likely to have a positive experience, even if you never have another date with this person. When your date explains his or her job to you, you might learn something useful that applies to your career. If he or she has a hobby that you know nothing about, again, you might pick up some information that you'll remember for the rest of your life. Look for those gems even if within the first thirty seconds of the date you're pretty sure that this person isn't someone with whom you're going to fall in love. By bringing some passion to your search, you're more likely to be rewarded.

Basically a first date is a little like that porridge for the three bears in *Goldilocks and the Three Bears*: you don't want your attitude to be too hot or too cold but just right.

Having a positive attitude will also help you in the future. After you learn to make the most of a date with someone who isn't quite right for you, imagine how much better the experience will be when that person sitting across from you is someone you really want to get to know a lot better. Don't bring a dark cloud of gloom with you that your date will have to figure out how to dissolve so that you can shine through; instead, bring a sparkle that will highlight the best aspects of your date.

Let me repeat my definition of the word *date*, because it's important for you, my readers, to be on the same page as me. When I say "date," I'm talking about two people getting together in the hopes that a deeper relationship will develop. Those hopes may be high or low, but they're there, as opposed to getting together with a friend with whom you have no interest in developing a romantic relationship. Being on a date always has stakes, which means that even two people who've been dating a while but haven't made any commitments to one another might at some point run into some difficulty that puts their relationship in jeopardy, something that wouldn't have been a problem had they been merely friends. (When to have sex is one subject that comes to mind, but there are plenty of others.)

How do you deal with this inherent tension? Being a sweaty, nervous wreck isn't going to help the relationship move in the right direction. Here are some tips that should make it a bit easier.

I know that many of you, particularly women, worry about your looks foremost, but doing so is a mistake. That's not to say that your appearance isn't important, but you can only do so much to change the way you look. At 4′7″, I never even bothered to wear high heels, because what were a few more inches going to accomplish? Although you may think your blue dress makes you look thin, your date may hate the color blue, or be color-blind. That's why fussing too much with the way you look can be a waste of time. You do need to look your best, because you don't want to turn off your date and because looking your best may give you a tad more confidence. But if you spend too much time worrying about how you look—trying on a dozen different outfits, for example—it may mean you're not preparing in ways that will actually make the date more rewarding. Even if you're bored with your dating outfit, leave well enough alone, unless thinking about clothes keeps you from getting overly stressed out about the coming date. In that case, fuss to your heart's content.

Good conversation is the key to doing your part to make sure a date works well. Being a good conversationalist takes preparation. The first part of the conversation may be easy because you'll be exchanging your personal histories, and you should know yours backward and forward (including the parts you want to make sure to leave out!). If you have shared interests, then those might take up the "second act" of a first date's dialogue, but understand the fact that if you're both "aficionados," the conversation could get boring. You won't be bringing anything new to the table but rather rehashing what you both already know. For example, if you both read a lot of comics and rely on being able to talk for a long time about your favorite comic heroes, I can pretty much guarantee that the conversation will get awkward quickly. A conversation that is nothing more than a back-and-forth about how great that epic battle between superheroes in a particular comic book was is going to feel artificial after fifteen minutes or so, and you'll both sense that it's time to switch topics, which is when your preparation has to kick in.

By the way, whatever you do, don't try to show up the other person by proving that you know more than he or she does on this shared interest. On a first date you want to build up the other person's ego, not tear it down. Showing off like that is a sure way of not having a second date, not to mention if your date knows more than you do, your attempt at showing off could completely backfire.

If you're prepared to talk about another subject, then you can move the conversation in the direction that you want it to go. If you're not, then maybe your date will take the lead, and it might be down a path you'd prefer not to wander, which is why, as in chess, it's better to make the first move.

For example, assume you went to a community college, lived at home, and always had one or more part-time jobs to pay for school, so your social life during those years wasn't anything like that shown in movies about college life. The last place you want the conversation to head, then, is your college experience and how much fun it was to go to all those sorority and fraternity parties, because you never did. But say you've discovered that one comic-book writer or artist lives or lived near you. Using that information you can steer the conversation from comics to talk about your neighborhood and all its quirks, and ask questions about where your date grew up. You'll be covering new yet safe ground, making for an interesting conversational interlude.

Obviously if you keep dating this individual, you're going to have to share what happened to you during your college years. But if talking about those years will tear down your self-confidence somewhat, then stay away from the topic, as much as possible, on a first date. I'm giving you one example, because after all, I can't outline every possible scenario my readers might have, but I hope you get the idea so that you'll look at your life history and plan out ways to talk about those topics in which you will shine.

What happens if your date is one of those people who hasn't had one interesting thing happen to him or her since college and so keeps going back to that subject? If you've been pushing the conversation away from college and he or she hasn't picked up on that, then you know this person either isn't perceptive or is too wrapped up in him or herself. But if you're forced into a topic that isn't your strongest suit, because it's only a first date, stop fighting it and go with the flow. It may guarantee that there will never be a second date, which is a possibility that exists on any first date.

I used the phrase "conversational interlude," and you should keep that concept in your head. Most conversations wander from topic to topic, and you have to develop a sense of when it's time to make such a switch. Certainly if you've run out of things to say on a particular topic, steering it in another direction would be to your benefit. But you won't be able to do that if you're not prepared.

Do you just jump in to start a new topic? You can. Conversations often have pauses, so if you're ready to head in a new direction, just wait for one of those pauses and steer the conversation in some new direction. You can't do it ten times in an hour without looking like a scatterbrain, but you most certainly can do it once or twice. And while doing it, look into the other person's eyes. Being looked at like that will distract your date a bit, and hopefully he or she won't even notice what you just did to nudge the path of your conversation into a new area.

To arm yourself with conversational fodder, keep up with current events, because somewhere in the news is a topic that likely will arise in a first conversation. If it's political and controversial, you can say, if you'd prefer, "I'd rather not talk about politics. Let's get to know one another a little better first." But if some recent tragedy has been splashed across the front pages or a kitten was rescued or whatever else is in the headlines, you should make a point of knowing something about it so that you can comment intelligently. And maybe try to check out news in categories that you don't usually follow, such as sports, business, or fashion. Surprise your date by showing that you're more well rounded than he or she might have guessed.

I'm going to put in a plug here for my favorite newspaper, the *New York Times*; you can read a certain number of articles online for free. The *Times* covers offbeat topics as well as hard news, so as a *Times* reader, you'll be more likely to have some ready-made conversation starters at hand.

Because you might have to wait for your date to show, especially if you arrive early so as not to be too nervous about being late, I suggest bringing along a book. Not only will it help you pass the time, but it also will be ready subject matter for your conversation. There's no easier way to start a conversation than saying, "Oh, what are you reading?" so some comment about the book you're holding is an opening that your date will likely adopt. (If you regularly read on your phone instead of on paper, I suggest making it a real book, because otherwise your date will have no idea that you were reading a book and not checking what I just posted to my Twitter feed!) Make sure the book is one that you haven't just started, or the discussion isn't likely to go far. Better yet, take a book that you've already read on subject matter that reflects one of your interests. That way you can be sure the conversation will be on familiar ground, and you can keep up your end without any trouble.

I know the more common way to pass time when waiting is to keep your eyes glued to your phone. One reason is so that you can immediately spot a text saying that your date is going to be late or not show up. But doing something a little unexpected, like reading a book, might make you stand out over other dates this person has had. Plus a book seems more serious, so if you're kept waiting, when this date apologizes for being late, your comeback can be "That's okay. I brought along a good book to read." That will make it seem like you're not that invested and will take Mr. or Ms. Fashionably Late down a notch.

These conversations are a balancing act. You want to be somewhat careful what you say so as to give off a good impression, but you also need to be paying close attention to what your date is saying—not just to keep the conversation flowing but also to learn as much as you can about him or her. You learn a lot about a person by noticing more than what he or she is saying, because we humans communicate in a variety of ways, including body language, intonation, etc. If your brain is too busy trying to come up with witty remarks, you might not pick up telltale signs of this other person's character traits.

Of course, you may know within the first five minutes of some dates that the person sitting across the table isn't the right one for you. Making small talk to extend this date is probably the last thing you want to do, but you also don't want to be rude. One solution is to use an app that rings your phone. You can set it up ahead of time so that it rings, say, fifteen minutes into your date. When your phone rings, you can either ignore it if the date is going well, or excuse yourself to answer it and then come back with an excuse you've practiced to get out of the date. If everybody uses this trick, it won't really serve its purpose—getting out of a date without being rude—because everyone's phone will ring fifteen minutes in. As a result, I advise to use this only when you have serious doubts about this person ahead of time.

Assuming that you're not immediately turned off by the person sitting across from you, be careful not to fall into the trap of being too formulaic, answering the typical questions about where you're from and what you do the same way on every date. If you're a Tinder veteran, for example, and have gone out on many introductory first dates, you might develop the tendency to answer all the initial questions as if you're reading a script. Doing so isn't going to show off your best side. If you find yourself drifting into a set story, find ways to change it up. We all have stories about some funny, poignant, or interesting events that took place during our lifetime. You should write them down so that they're well formulated and on the tip of your tongue.

Now suppose you're asked where you were born. Instead of answering directly, say something like "That's not interesting, but let me tell you about the time . . ." and go into one of these stories. Or you could make it into a quiz: "Guess whether it was Omaha, Nebraska; Brooklyn; or Pierre, South Dakota." No matter what answer your date gives you, ask why he or she chose it, which should get the conversation rolling nicely.

Or, instead of answering the same question with your birthplace, you could give your birth sign. Your date may initially respond quizzically, wondering whether you misheard the question or are teasing. His or her response will then be quite telling, no matter what it is. If you get an answer that shows some creativity, then that will be a good sign and the two of you can have some fun. If the person just repeats the question with a frown on his or her face and shows little imagination, then maybe that will be a sign that this date won't work out. Such challenges will wake up your brain a bit, and your level of alertness will show on your face. Otherwise your body language might make you look bored, even though you're actually bored by your own responses.

By the way, some of the tips I've just given might be especially relevant to someone who is a bit shy. The better prepared you are, the less likely you'll wind up tongue-tied. Another way to prepare is to have some interesting questions ready, maybe a question your date has never heard before. Instead of asking, "What's your birth sign?" you can try "What's your favorite planet?" Don't ask what high school he or she attended but rather what science project he or she did in elementary school. After a conversation gets going, it becomes a lot easier to keep it going, even though in the beginning it can be awkward. If you offer up a question, you can choose one for which you have an interesting reply. If your sixth-grade class had a funny kid, then ask your date what his or her favorite middle school class was. Then when it's your turn to answer, you'll have an entertaining story to share. Remember that conversation is an art. If you were a ballerina, you'd need to prepare and practice to get better. Conversing is no different. If you think you're bad at it, then rest assured you need more preparation and practice, so get started now.

Some of you may be thinking, *Come on, Dr. Ruth, this sounds too contrived. I think people should just be themselves.* For people who are good at dating, that may be true. But they probably would not be reading a book such as this. And then there's the matter of context. If you're dating solely to have a good time—to have a one-night stand for example—then preparation is less important. But if you're on a search for the love of your life, why not prepare? That way, if fate hands you the opportunity to land that person, you'll be ready.

As I've said, body language is an integral part of the message you convey. Even if you suddenly can't think of anything to say, instead of looking down at your lap for inspiration, look the other person in the eye and give a big smile. That smile won't quite replace a flow of words, but it will help you get through this rough spot.

Some people say to themselves, *My life is so boring. What can I possibly talk about?* Such negative thoughts aren't going to help you. But if that's what you believe, then maybe before you even start dating, you need to liven up your life. Here's a simple suggestion. You have to eat, so instead of eating boring things, look up recipes and make interesting meals for yourself. If there's one thing you can be sure of is that your date eats, and so if you can talk about food, you'll have his or her attention.

Other things you can do are attend popular movies, take classes, read articles online or in magazines, listen to some popular podcasts, or watch some TED Talks. By the way, you can take many college classes on your own schedule for free on your computer without leaving your home.

A standard topic of conversation is what you do to earn a living. What if what you do from nine to five is boring and you hate it and can't wait to move on? The answer is to talk about your ambitions. Everyone has taken a job out of necessity in order to put a roof over their heads and some food on the table. When I first came to the United States, I was a housekeeper earning a big seventy-five cents an hour. Before that I had worked on a kibbutz picking tomatoes under the hot sun for nothing more than permission to sleep in a tent and some leftover food. I wanted to be a kindergarten teacher, and I told everyone I met about my ambition. At one point I met someone who helped me get to Jerusalem to study teaching. And I didn't remain a housekeeper for long here in the United States.

Having a life plan is not only helpful when furthering this first-date conversation, it also will help you hold your head high in all social situations. What you do at the moment doesn't matter as long as you're headed toward a goal. But if all you can say is "I hate my job," then the person you're meeting for the first time will wonder what type of person you are. So show some ambition, not just on these dates but also in your life.

Bear in mind that the overall impression you make will be based on a few standout moments. If you keep looking at the glass in front of you with a scared look on your face, then that's what your date is going to remember. But if you speak passionately about something, even for only a few minutes, more than likely your date will remember you for that. You don't have full control over what happens during a date, but you have some, so to use it to your best advantage you need to be prepared.

Rather than being shy, some people talk too much, especially if they're nervous. If you know that you're one of them, then force yourself to stop talking every once in a while and listen instead. Having some silence during a conversation is okay. If you've been talking a blue streak, your date might even welcome it. Another way to stop yourself from hogging the conversation is to ask a question, which will give your date the floor, so to speak. Handing over the mic is important if you notice a bored expression on the other person's face. That will tell you that you're talking too much and that if you want to salvage this date, you're going to have to make a conscious effort to talk less.

People who are lonely often end up talking too much when they finally get the chance. That scenario tells your date two things: you have difficulties getting dates, and you have a tendency to talk too much. Before having this date I suggest that you talk to someone else, perhaps a friend or your mother, on the phone for a while. Who you talk to doesn't matter. Just pour your heart out and get this need of yours to talk somewhat satisfied, so that you'll be ready to do your share of listening on this date.

We all have faults, some of which are minor and some of which are of greater consequence. If you have one or two dates that don't pan out, but others seem to go fine, then don't worry about your faults too much. If all your dates go badly, then spend some time on introspection. Think about what happened on your last date and figure out where it might have gone off the rails. If the cause is something that's under your control, then try and fix whatever it is.

You might also ask some friends for their opinion. Maybe you're someone who doesn't care so much about appearance, which is okay to a point, but perhaps your dates don't want to be seen with someone whose wardrobe hasn't been updated in a decade. Or maybe you curse too much or rely too much on humor, so you're giving your dates the impression that you don't have a serious side. Whatever it might be, a good friend can tell you what you might be doing wrong. You might not like hearing your friend's opinion, but pay attention and then make an attempt to change according to what you've been told, assuming that you want your dating results to improve.

When I was a young girl, I was sure nobody would ever want to date me. (That I was a poor, short orphan didn't help either.) I was able to compensate for my height in other ways and so learned how to attract male attention and was married three times. Given my experience, I think I'm qualified to give some advice to all those who are less than perfect physically, meaning those who are overweight, have bad skin, stammer, limp, or whatever.

Let me share how I met my third husband, Fred, to whom I was married for thirty-five years before he passed away. I had gone skiing with a tall friend. When we rode the T-bar lift up the mountain, we weren't a good fit. When we got to the top, I was introduced to a much shorter man. I told my friend, "From now on I'm going up the T-bar with this short one." That short guy turned out to be Fred.

As this story illustrates, I took charge of the situation. I spotted someone who seemed like a good fit, and I didn't wait to see what might develop but forged ahead on my own. I could have been rejected, but I wasn't. And I used every trick I could think of from that moment on to make sure that I didn't lose Fred. I'm tempted to say that Fred never stood a chance, but that's not true. Rivals were after him, and I had to work hard to make sure that I was the one he chose. If he had rejected me, I would have been sad, but if I hadn't put in the extra effort, I probably would never have married him.

If you have some perceived fault, don't let it be an excuse for you to be a wallflower, but rather use it as motivation to push yourself as far out onto every limb as you can (keeping yourself safe, of course). If you manage to get a first date with someone online, and this other person strikes you as a possible match, then charge full steam ahead. Use every wile you possess to make this person like you, and hopefully whatever it is that you have that would be an impediment to getting to that second date becomes so tiny in this other person's eyes that he or she completely overlooks it.

Let me be clear about one thing. I'm not telling you to use sex to accomplish such goals. Whether to have sex is a separate decision. Using sex as a lure will probably backfire, because some people will use you for sex and then dump you, so instead of developing a relationship you might develop a reputation. I understand that some people might think that by having sex on a first or second date, they will be able to keep this other person interested, but generally that's not the correct approach. Sex is something that two people can share, but it should take place within a relationship. If it's early on and there is no relationship, then it's too early to be having sex.

First dates don't automatically lead to marriage or even a second date, so keep your expectations at the level a first date deserves. If you go on a lot of first dates because some app keeps setting you up, you can easily get into the habit of making snap decisions. For instance, say you date three brunettes in a row, and they all go badly. You might say to yourself, *I'm not a fan of brunettes* and pass them all by. But that is putting the blame where it doesn't belong, because hair color should never be a deciding factor. Basing your decision on minutiae means you could end up with a series of first dates, or even no dates, and nothing more.

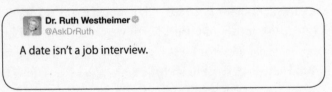

Dr. Ruth Westheimer ✔
@AskDrRuth

A date isn't a job interview.

Remember that a date isn't a job interview. During a job interview you're trying to prove yourself because you want to be hired. You know you're competing against other people for this job, and you're also aware that what this potential employer is looking for is specific and job related. You may be a well-rounded individual, but if you're not an ace at Excel, for example, then your odds of getting this job are nil. On the other hand, the dating game requires that you're well rounded rather than singularly focused.

Although I tell you to put your imagination, dry wit, and street vocabulary on the shelf during a job interview, that's not necessarily the case during a date. Don't exaggerate any of these traits right away; you need to get a better sense of the other person before you really open up. But unlike a job interview, a date should be fun, so put some effort at making it so.

Furthermore, job interviews should have zero sexual content. (If a prospective employer is propositioning you, get up and leave.) If you're interested in the person you're dating and sharing some time, then you're allowed to be a bit sexy. However, make sure that you don't exaggerate this aspect, because you risk scaring the other person off. If he or she hasn't warmed up to you enough to give any thought to having sex with you, then coming off too sexy could be a huge mistake. You're still allowed to flirt to some extent. You can give compliments, as long as they're not sickeningly sweet, and some casual physical contact might be within bounds.

<u>Stop and Consider:</u> **If you're not good at reading other people, then keep the sexy quotient turned off.**

One problem with sex—and I say men are more guilty of this than women—is that it can turn you into someone with a one-track mind. I'm all for having some sexuality show through on a first date if it remains in the context of flirting. But if you go any further and make what might be read as a proposition, you've probably crossed a line that you shouldn't. Some people are good at seeing how the person they're talking to reacts, while others can be blinded by what's going on inside their own head, and if it has to do with sex, then that's especially true. If you think that your flirtatious behavior could cause the exact opposite effect of what you seek, then don't go there.

Some people use an app like Tinder or Grindr just to look for sex. Doing so isn't wise, but that's an individual decision. A one-night stand arranged on Tinder isn't likely to lead to a long-term, loving relationship, and finding that is the subject of this book. If all you want is sex, just be careful and bear in mind that you're putting off the best part that human sexuality can bring, which is the love that two people share. Being a couple for a night isn't the same thing as being a couple. But if that's all you want, so be it.

While looking into your date's eyes is important because it shows you're giving this other person your full attention, if you're a man on a date with a woman and she's wearing a plunging neckline, then you have to be careful about staring. I know the argument, "If she didn't want me to look, why wear something suggestive?" I didn't tell you not to look; just don't stare. And ladies, dressing too sexy on a first date is a mistake. What makes a game of strip poker sexy is how undressing becomes a slow process. If you arrive at the poker table already naked, what's the point? And it's the same with dating. The longer it takes to go from meeting to having sex, the more intense the experience will be when it happens, so dress for a timetable that isn't later that night. If you're headed to some bar and you want to attract the most men to come over and offer to buy you a drink, then dressing sexy might be the right thing to do, but don't do that on a first date.

There's been a lot in the news over the years about the various drugs that could be slipped into someone's drink to make him or her an unwilling sex partner, so people obviously have to be careful about the risk of that happening to them. Drinking too much alcohol can lead to the same problem. First dates can be nerve-wracking, and many people feel the need for some alcohol in the system to get them through the experience. Seeing someone walk into a bar, order a shot, quickly down it, and then quietly nurse a beer or glass of wine is a good sign that this person is waiting for a first date. But too much alcohol will also make it much harder to judge the person you're dating. You'll be in a bit of a fog and probably won't remember many details the next day. I'm all for you having a glass of wine or beer, but unless you decide while not under the influence that this person is worth spending a lot more time with, don't order that second drink (or just sip it very slowly). That way you can make an accurate decision about whether you want to go on another date with this person.

<u>Stop and Consider:</u> What are the financial ramifications of first dates?

Because first dates usually take place in public places like bars and restaurants where there is a cost, if you go on a lot of dates, the price of admission to the dating world can be high, especially for guys who have a tendency to pick up the tab. Because you can never know how a first date is going to go, my advice is to keep it simple. Don't make it a dinner date. If you decide that you want to spend more time together, you can always agree to go to dinner (and potentially also agree to split the tab), but if you meet at a bar or coffee shop, then your investment will be minimal. Be prepared to split the tab, but if your date insists on paying, let him pick up the first drink or cup of java. If you have a second round, then you can agree to pay. And if you're spending so much time enjoying your evening together that there's going to be a third alcoholic beverage, then make sure that you eat something so you don't get drunk. Otherwise you might do something you'll regret. For the first drink that your date is probably going to buy, order a beer or glass of wine rather than some fancy, expensive cocktail. Your concern for your date's wallet will be appreciated.

One type of encounter you may run into is with an alcoholic. While an alcoholic may be interested in a relationship, finding someone to buy them drinks might actually be the main purpose. I spoke with one young man who took a woman out to a wine bar, and she proceeded to chug seven glasses, leaving him with quite a tab and the need to get her safely back to her apartment. No matter how chivalrous you may be, if your date is getting drunk, before the situation gets out of hand, I'd say it's all right to leave some cash on the table for your drinks and walk away.

Even if you're at a place that serves liquor, you can order something nonalcoholic. Alcohol sometimes can make it easier to talk, but it dulls your senses, so it might lessen your ability to judge another person. You don't have to be a teetotaler and not drink alcohol on a first date, but you shouldn't feel forced to order alcohol just because the other person does. Anyone who doesn't want to be stuck with a huge bar bill just needs to find places to meet where alcohol isn't served.

I see other advantages of having a first date someplace where liquor isn't served, like a coffee shop. Choosing to meet at a coffee shop makes you appear a bit more serious right off the bat. It sends the message that you're not going out with this person just to have a good time but that you want to meet and learn more about him or her. Because places that serve alcohol are often noisier, with loud music and intoxicated people, you would both likely have to raise your voices to talk, which makes it more difficult to get an accurate impression of each other. If you're sitting at a quiet table in a coffee shop, you're more likely to see the real him or her. If you're having a good time and then want to go to a bar, fine, but you don't have to start out meeting at one.

Make sure that wherever you meet is a public place, preferably with several exits. Creeps exist in the dating world, and you don't want to find yourself cornered by one.

Here are some other safety tips:

- Tell one or two other people, friends or family, that you're going on a first date, where you're going to be, and maybe some contact information for this person you're meeting, such as his or her handle on the dating site.
- Make sure that your cell phone is charged and ready to use if needed.
- If you didn't choose the location, check out the neighborhood of the place you're meeting on Google Maps, so if you have to leave quickly, you know where you are.
- If you drive to the meeting, park someplace where your car is well lit. If your date asks you to meet someplace that is in a sketchy neighborhood, don't be afraid to insist on another venue.

Although this type of safety advice may apply more to my women readers, men shouldn't underestimate the risks. They, too, might be lured to a nearby hotel, drugged, and then robbed. Granted, scenarios happen much less frequently to men, but they're still a possibility if you're not careful. And the more you brag about your financial stature online, the more likely that you'll be made the target of a criminal.

Although alcohol can help loosen your inhibitions, you don't want to let alcohol or your ego turn you into somebody you're not. Yes, you're putting your best foot forward, but don't don some sort of mask in an attempt to hide the real you. Don't brag or put on airs or act in any way that might lead this person you're dating to get the wrong picture. Why not? Because if you two do hit it off, you don't want to have to act like you're somebody else each time you get together in the future.

Actually, any lie you tell could come back to haunt you. You don't have to be completely honest, but I suggest that if you're going to be playing a bit loose with the truth, make it more an act of omission than commission. You can keep your dirty laundry safely locked away for this first date and many dates thereafter, but if you tell an outright lie, you're likely to trip yourself up at some point, and then you could lose this person just when the relationship is developing nicely.

<u>Stop and Consider:</u> It's okay to edit your life story, but if you embellish it with lies, eventually those lies will come back to haunt you.

One problem heterosexual men have with dating apps is how the opposite sex is much more selective, which narrows the man's field of choice. In other words, a woman who is using one of these apps to find a man is likely to get many more men asking her to go out than the other way around. Men have always had to deal with rejection, but on one of these dating apps the number of negative swipes might end up being quite depressing. I've read that in such cases, a picture that shows the man doing something, rather than a simple headshot, is more appealing, so I urge my male readers who struggle with this to carefully select their photos so that more women will give them a positive swipe. If you're not sure which type of photos work best, do some research. Look for information on the web from experts and ask your female friends what they think of the pictures that you are considering posting.

Another dating scenario might occur if someone you know casually, such as from work or the neighborhood, says, "I have tickets to such-and-such a show. Would you like to go with me?" Since that person has selected the event and invited you, then he or she should pay. That situation is straightforward. But what if you'd been looking at this person who asked you out in a positive light but the event itself is one you don't particularly want to attend? You only have a second or two to respond, so what do you say?

If the event would make you uncomfortable—say extremely loud, obnoxious music—then you have to make up an excuse. After all, this invitation is for a specific date, so you could be booked. But unless you would hate attending this event, I advise going. Why? Because if this person has two tickets, he or she is probably going to ask someone else.

This person could ask a friend, or he or she could ask a potential rival date. If you're interested in this person, don't let this opportunity slip away, because you might not get another one.

I believe in being strategic. Let me tell you a story from my dating days. I was dating my future husband Fred, but he was also seeing some other women, including one who especially had his attention. Fred played the guitar, and he accidentally left his guitar at this other woman's apartment. Because I didn't want him going back there, and even though as a single mother I was poor as the proverbial church mouse, I took a friend who knew something about guitars to a musical instrument store and bought Fred a new one. I didn't just hope he'd never go back to her apartment—I took action to ensure that he didn't have a built-in excuse. Because Fred and I did eventually marry, you can see my plan worked, though I guess I can't prove that if he had gone back he wouldn't have married me anyway. But that wasn't the only time I did all I could to make Fred mine, and my point is don't be afraid to be as proactive as possible if you have a "live" one on the line.

Dr. Ruth Westheimer ✔
@AskDrRuth

First dates should be solo affairs.

Some people bring along a friend or two on first dates, possibly for safety reasons or just for some extra eyes and ears to vet the date. If you don't trust yourself to judge whether your date is worthy of your time, then maybe you're not ready for dating. Young teens date in packs, but after you get beyond your teen years, dating should be a two-person affair. Going out in groups is a bit problematic, because it doesn't teach you how to behave when you're one-on-one. How do you learn to hold up your end of a conversation when you have nobody to turn to? And the whole demeanor of a group is different than a couple: more boisterous with more jokes and less intimacy. And what about how you'll feel sharing a meal sitting right across from someone to whom you're attracted and who might make your stomach tighten up a bit? You can't have your posse with you all the time, no matter how much comfort they bring you. They're not going to join you in bed when you first have sex with this person, are they? The time to cut the apron strings is at the beginning of the relationship. Not only must you be able to stand on your own two feet, but also you have to recognize the risk that this date of yours might decide that one of your friends is more to his or her liking, and then you might lose a potential partner and probably a friend as well.

The most important reason for you to be alone for this first meeting is you have to be able to concentrate on the person in front of you and the discussion you share. You're going to have a lot of distractions. I've mentioned your own brain, which will be thinking of your answers and trying to hone them so they are as interesting as possible. Doing this will undeniably make it harder to really listen to this other person. (Some women like the security of having a friend along when meeting a new man, which is understandable, but your bodyguard doesn't have to be sitting at the same table as you or the next barstool. He or she can be someplace else, at a different table or the other end of the bar, and if after a while all seems to be going well, you can give your friend a sign so he or she can leave.)

Completely ignoring your surroundings and what is going on around you in the bar, restaurant, park, or wherever you meet is impossible. Sometimes a distraction, like a waitress spilling a drink, allows for a moment of comedy, which could be a good thing. But if either of you is constantly looking around, checking out who else is there, then you're too easily distracted, which perhaps is an indication that this person isn't holding your interest and isn't the right one for you.

On the other hand, some people find that having a built-in distraction on a first date is a good idea. First dates are always awkward, but if you're doing something together, like playing mini golf or bowling, then the game will take the edge off your nervousness. If that's a conscious decision, then I approve. But if you're acting distracted when you shouldn't be, that's not a good thing.

A date that involves an activity allows the two of you to interact about whatever you're doing. When you're in a place conducive only to talking, much of the conversation will center on past events in both of your histories. But if you're sharing an activity like climbing a rock wall, exploring antique shops, or visiting a local winery, then the activity will provide you with fresh situations where you can make spontaneous comments and show off your wit. Someone telling you his or her history may be able to get away with well-rehearsed lines, but when you're sharing an activity, you're almost guaranteed to see the person in a different light. You'll each react instantaneously to what's going on, which will give you better insights into each other's character than just posing questions.

You'll also be creating bonds. If you've been on fifty dates at a bar, they'll all blend together; however, if your first date is at a bowling alley, the games will help to cement your relationship. I'm not saying that just because you bowled together that you're bound to fall in love. What I am saying is that the date will stand out in your memory more than others. If this date isn't someone you feel has potential, the date itself might be more enjoyable, because at least you were playing a game rather than making a game out of conversation.

Another potential distraction is going to be your past love interests. And in this Tinder age, that topic is likely to include the many other people with whom you've had a first date, possibly dozens, maybe even more. This offers two ways of distracting you. The first is to compare this new person to your past dates. The other distraction is the temptation to start thinking beyond this date, whether you already have any such dates arranged or not. If the first few minutes have been a bit awkward, then you might be quicker to cross this date off than you might be if you didn't know you could look at the app and choose from hundreds of other people.

Sometimes the distractions won't matter, and sometimes they'll even serve a purpose. If someone has lied in your communications through the online dating app, and once you're in person, you can almost instantly tell that he or she isn't the person you thought, or someone you would want to get serious with, then you're excused from being distracted. But if this person isn't that far off from the picture that you had painted in your head, then you owe it to him or her to stay focused, in part because you want this individual to be equally respectful of you.

Although not having many opportunities to date is certainly a problem, having too many opportunities to date turns out to create problems as well. Instead of trying to make a relationship work, the vast pool of potential other people to date will push you the other way. Why try to look under the surface of this person you're currently with to discover hidden assets when maybe someone else in this constant flow of dates you have might be incrementally better?

Every couple, not just those dating but also those married for decades, has encountered the pull of all the attractive people around them. Why make a continued investment in your current partner when there are, as the saying goes, so many fish in the sea (and people whose availability has increased incrementally thanks to all these apps)? Developing a loving relationship takes time. Over time that relationship brings many rewards that are unavailable to someone who is always playing the field. Even if you're fully aware that what you're looking for is real love, the temptations of the current dating scene can make keeping that goal front and center difficult. The two people dating each other have to share this goal and be equally committed to the relationship.

We live in an era when everything moves extremely fast, and people's attention spans have become shorter. No remote control device can change channels in real life. Arriving at a rewarding life is a step-by-step process, and if you never choose one path, you'll end up running in circles instead of getting ahead.

<u>Stop and Consider:</u> Are you a keeper?

On a first date make yourself as desirable as possible. Be attentive, smile, look into the other person's eyes, and work at keeping the conversation going. In other words, be that ideal date, even if after only five minutes you're pretty sure that you don't want to date this person again. First of all, maybe if this person is put at ease, he or she will open up and you'll discover a pearl in that oyster shell. But even if you don't, by practicing your best dating skills you'll be making yourself a better candidate, what some would call a keeper, when you do meet that special someone. Also, allowing yourself to fall into being grouchy and miserable could turn into a bad habit that you'll have a hard time kicking later on. And finally, if you do a good job at making the evening as pleasant as possible, at the end you might discover that you didn't have a bad time at all, and, if nothing else, you entertained yourself, so whether you ever see this person again, the date won't have been a total waste of time.

How effective you are at making your best effort to be that ideal date will depend on many factors. Without a doubt, the baggage you bring to it will be an important one. By "baggage," I mean your psychological makeup, which could make this first date more difficult. One common and potentially influential piece of baggage is any recent relationship you've had. Whether you broke up with this past lover or he or she broke up with you (or worse, this person passed away), this person is likely to "accompany" you on this first date. He or she will pop into your thoughts before, during, and after this date. It's inevitable, even if you tell yourself a thousand times that you're not going to compare this date with your past lover.

The longer this past relationship lasted, the more you loved this other person, and the harder the breakup, the more it's going to affect you in the present. To be on a date necessitates that you be at least somewhat emotionally vulnerable. If you were to shut down all your emotions, this other person would only see a stone-cold version of the real you and in all likelihood never want to see you again. Hence, you have to allow the real you to shine through, but the real you includes the emotions that you underwent during this past relationship.

If all you can think of is the pain at the end of the relationship, then you're going to have a difficult time during this first date. You're going to be gun-shy, afraid that you might get hurt again, which is reasonable, but feeling that way won't be helpful and won't put you at your best. Somehow you have to include memories of the good times you had with this past lover, memories that will make you want to share tender moments with someone new, possibly even the person sitting across from you.

Dr. Ruth Westheimer ✔
@AskDrRuth

Remember the good times.

We humans aren't in full control of our emotions, and so we have a tendency to want to shut out the bad ones. The problem is that when you force your emotions into a locked box, you also stow away the good ones. If you want to love again, by necessity you have to feel the pain of a past relationship as well. The mourning period serves as a time when this pain is more acute. As it slowly loses its intensity, it will be easier for you to love someone else. But failing to mourn and forcing all your emotions out of your consciousness in order not to feel the pain will only lead to you losing your ability to love altogether.

How long should this mourning period be? Although it shouldn't go on for too long, there's no minimum. Some people meet someone new right after a severe breakup, and the relationship works out fine, whereas others absolutely need longer to adjust. Accept that it's temporary, and don't allow the pain of mourning to take over your life. You have to move on physically and emotionally. Let the pain envelope you for a time, but as soon as you can, start to break free from it so that you can meet someone new.

By the way, letting go may also mean letting go of actual possessions. The following example led me to get my apartment redone! Nate Berkus asked me to come on his show to give some advice. A young woman was having problems enjoying sex with her new boyfriend in part because all her bedroom furniture, which she had shared with her former boyfriend, reminded her of him, and so she couldn't relax fully with her new man. I told her that as soon as she got home she should call the Salvation Army and have them take it all away. Better to sleep on a mattress on the floor than have this new relationship ruined by furniture that carried so many memories.

How did this advice get me an apartment makeover? Well, my apartment needed a lot of work, and while standing on the TV stage with Nate Berkus after answering the young woman's question, for which I got a nice round of applause from the audience, I asked Nate if he would redo my apartment. He said yes. Of course, he filmed the whole thing, and you can find it on the internet. My reaction when I saw what a fabulous job he did is priceless.

Getting over losing a lover is admittedly more difficult if you're a widow or widower and the marriage lasted a long time. After your partner dies, you're left with a much deeper void. It's not just a question of getting rid of some old pieces of furniture. Healing will take longer, but you will heal, and the sooner there's a special someone to speed that process up, the better.

Widows and widowers also have to learn to deal with guilt as well as grief. Feeling that you're cheating on your spouse who passed away when you date someone new is natural. On the other hand, some widows and widowers actually feel that their dearly departed actually played a role in finding them someone new, and who knows, maybe that's so. That attitude is certainly the right one to have. It's sad enough when a spouse dies, but allowing that sadness to fester for the rest of your life would be a big mistake. If a crutch like believing that your spouse has arranged this new match for you is effective at blocking out the guilt, then go right ahead and indulge.

Dr. Ruth Westheimer ●
@AskDrRuth

Dating is hard.

I wish I could offer up easy answers to all the questions you might have before a first date, but there are too many for me to get to each one. If you're lucky, dating can quickly lead into a serious relationship, but sometimes you endure long stretches where dating is hard. Convince yourself that the potential results are worth it. To tell your friends or yourself that you're not interested in dating, just to avoid the difficulties of dating, is a mistake. The rewards of a loving relationship are worth the effort.

4.

Is This Going Well?

Your first date together has ended. You're sitting on your bed trying to figure out what to make of the evening. You're analyzing your emotions while guessing your date's. In many cases, they're both hard to decipher.

That you're not sure of how you feel about your date—and you're even less certain of how your date feels about you—explains why your emotions are mixed. Even if you were sure you never wanted to date this person again, you wouldn't want to think that you were being rejected, but because at this point you don't yet know how he or she feels about you, your reaction is going to be somewhat confused by this uncertainty.

People are complex, and you can't possibly know enough about someone you just met. If this person doesn't have some layers to peel back, then I say there was something wrong, that he or she lacked depth to the extent that you'd quickly get bored with each other. So even though you do have a picture, it's not complete, which makes sorting out how you feel about him or her more difficult.

After a first date, sometimes you're absolutely certain that you want a second, but other times you might not be sure yet. More than likely your attitude is going to be wait and see. And equally likely your date is no more certain than you are. But you hope that he or she wants to explore the chemistry between the two of you a little more.

Assume that after this first date, you want to go on another date with this person. And perhaps, when you parted company, it may have seemed like the two of you would have another date in your future, but then it never happened. Did you completely misread what took place? Was your date a good actor, making you think that all went well when clearly he or she didn't think so? Or did you just miss all the signs that were there so that your expectations of another date were way out of proportion?

You'll probably never know the answer to these questions. I'd like to tell you not to waste your time pondering the imponderable, but I know human nature well enough to understand that would be almost impossible. And the debriefing you're going to give yourself, or maybe your friends, serves a purpose. You might learn some valuable lessons about your dating skills from dates that go nowhere, and so forgetting what happened the minute the date is over would be foolish. And that's true even of dates where you instantaneously knew it was never going to work, because then you have to question why you agreed to the date in the first place.

A quick analysis is an integral part of the dating game, but the key word is *quick*. A bad date is going to trigger some emotions, but they'll soon dissipate, assuming you let them. But if you keep returning to what occurred on this date, allowing the negative aspects to fester, then you'll be giving this bad date a lot more of your intellect, emotions, and, most importantly, time than it deserves. In a day or two, you have to put this date entirely behind you, or else it will have a negative impact on your future dates.

If all your dates are turning out badly, then you need to analyze your dating technique more intensely. And you might need to look beyond your skills. Perhaps the problem is the source of your dates. Are you using only one app to get these dates? That might suggest that you need to broaden your methods of searching. If the dates are coming from a variety of sources, then you have to look inward to see what you're doing wrong, because if your batting average is really low, then you're at least partly to blame.

One mistake people commonly make in dating is to lock in on one factor when deciding whether someone is worthy of a second date. Some men might decide that they only want to date a woman whose looks they feel meet a certain arbitrary rating, such as an 8, 9, or 10. Women might insist that their dates be taller than they are and muscular. I'm not talking about broad categories that will include lots of potential partners, such as having a college degree or being in a certain age range. Rather I'm focusing on selection factors that narrow the field considerably. The problem with narrowing the field by a factor such as appearance is that many who fit the category of beautiful or handsome are also vain. I'm not saying all, but a higher proportion. And too much vanity is usually accompanied by a surplus of self-centeredness, so if you're also looking for a partner who will be devoted to you, you'll find yourself struggling to get both qualities by such a narrow search.

Your search field might indicate a narrowness on your part as well. If you think that your partner's looks are critical, then you may be self-centered and so not all that loveable.

Ignoring appearance is more difficult when your initial search is on an app that requires swiping. I urge you to not swipe in just milliseconds based on the photo on your phone. First, doing so turns the use of these apps into more of a video game than a real search. But it's not a game! You're searching for a loving companion who will change your life forever. Force yourself to slow down the process. Look at what the people who've posted these pictures have written. Think about what they have to say and search for the qualities you're really looking for that are in their words. Stop making your eyes the main focus of your search and instead use your entire mind. Teach yourself to spot the qualities that really matter in the long run. If you meet someone and stay together for the next fifty years, appearances won't end up meaning much. When weighing whether to swipe left or right, don't limit yourself to appearance. Dig deeper.

<u>Stop and Consider:</u> **The qualities you want in a long-term partner aren't just surface deep, so why would you judge people to see if they're worth dating only by their appearance?**

Judging people by appearance isn't something people do only on dating apps. If you're at a social event, undoubtedly you're being judged and judging others by their appearance as well. What often happens is that as the evening goes on, people's standards go down. Someone they might not have been interested in earlier because of his or her appearance may become more attractive after a couple of hours of meeting nobody. What that shows is that your standards actually aren't as narrow as you may believe them to be. That realization should lead you to broaden your search pattern from the start. Some diamonds in the rough are undoubtedly out there, and the sooner you choose to meet them, the more likely that somebody else won't have taken them. That other information besides appearance is available on an app search is an asset you should use to your advantage. In turn, make sure that the information you put on any dating sites shows you off in the best light.

When deciding whether to go beyond that first date, some people get hung up on other broad categories in addition to appearance, including their date's profession, income level, and family background. Because I was short and an orphan you might say that for me to bring this up is sour grapes, but really, I'm being scientific. If you narrow down the pool of eligible partners too radically, given that other factors such as personality, intellect, and personal values end up being more important, you may find it very difficult to meet with success.

What do you do when this person you've just met takes your breath away? It does happen—the French call it *le coup de foudre*, the lightning bolt. One problem with such lightning bolts is that sometimes only one of you is hit. Then there you are, madly in love with someone who, at least outwardly, doesn't seem all that enamored with you.

In these types of situations you have to keep your cool. Why? First of all, you have to protect your heart to some extent. You don't want to give it free rein until you're sure that such feelings are going to be reciprocated. And then if you're acting lovesick in front of someone who clearly isn't feeling the same flames, you're going to appear foolish and so not your best. Be careful not to start gushing over this other person's every word. If you think that at such a moment you might say the wrong thing, then I suggest not saying too much at all. Smile, make eye contact, nod, pinch yourself under the table—do whatever works—but in cases where your emotions are getting carried away, remember that what you say could spoil everything, so bottle up some of those thoughts that are filling your head.

Love at first sight or not, assuming you do want to see him or her again, the first big set of questions that will be looming over you is who makes first contact, how, and when?

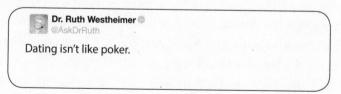

Dr. Ruth Westheimer ✓
@AskDrRuth

Dating isn't like poker.

When you're playing a card game, remember to shield the cards in your hand so that the other players can't see them. Many people use similar tactics when dating. They act like dating is a game and someone is going to win or lose. But as you might have guessed by now, I'm an impatient person. And in dating, I think there are good reasons not to play such waiting games.

Say this person you just shared drinks with is a little unsure of how he or she feels about you. Perhaps it's an extremely busy time in his or her life. Although he or she might want to contact you at some point, doing so isn't a priority. But if a week goes by, all that waiting could drive you up the wall, and it's possible someone else will come along to catch this person's eye, thus derailing your chances. Whatever your gender, if you're interested, communicate something. It could be just a simple text—*Enjoyed the evening*—or it could be more. Just don't sit idly by.

If you don't get any reply, then you have a good idea of where you stand (unless you're being benched—more on that in the next chapter). If your simple text begets only a simple returned text, that's not going to tell you all that much, is it? But if this person doesn't respond in a positive way—with some enthusiasm, or better yet, a request to meet again—then that response is telling. It won't guarantee that you'll never see this person again, but the odds have decreased to the point where you absolutely can't invest any of your emotions.

The emotional content of dating is what makes it so tricky. If you didn't care at all who you were dating, then whether a particular date got back to you or not wouldn't matter. But you do care, and if you date someone that you end up liking, you're going to want to date that person again. If at the end of the date you haven't been given a clear signal as to whether or not this next date is going to occur, your thoughts are going to start buzzing, driving you crazy.

As I said before, and will probably say again, you can't stop your brain from zeroing in on a particular topic. What you can do, what I say you must do, is to forcefully push such thoughts out of your consciousness. Spending so much emotional energy wondering what's going to happen between the two of you next won't do you any good, so don't do it. Stay cool, calm, and collected. You can do that by think-ing of something else. For example, say you've been thinking about buying a new car. Even if you weren't seriously thinking about it, when thoughts about this person you dated visit you, push them aside by concentrating on whether you prefer a sedan or an SUV. You can also substitute with something else you want—where you want to go on your next vacation, or whether you want to spend the money to see your favorite band in concert. Think about anything but this person. To be successful at this sort of exercise, you have to be ready. You have to know what subject you're going to concentrate on so that you can do so easily and before thoughts of this person overwhelm your brain. Planning ahead is therefore a key ingredient to maintaining control over your emotional state.

What if you get a text a week later asking for another date and your reaction is, "I was forced to wait so I'm not going to respond right away." If that's your response, what that tells me is that you're playing a game and you're emotionally invested in it. It says you weren't in control of your emotions, and maybe you were actually thinking about this person quite a lot, asking yourself why you weren't hearing back. And now this text, when it arrives a week later, will kick up your emotions another notch or two. You'll sit around and think about how to respond. You'll call a friend or two and dis-cuss the situation and what you should do. And you certainly won't text back immediately, because your emotions will ensure that tit for tat is the right way to go.

<u>Stop and Consider:</u> **When you make a game out of dating, you're more likely to lose.**

If you had been able to keep your emotions in check, then when you got that text a week later, assuming that you hadn't lost interest in this person, you could give a simple response and set up another date.

Maybe not within the first ten minutes, because that would signal that you're overeager, but within a couple of hours. But if you let your emotions run wild, you'll suffer during this week before you get the text, then suffer again deciding what to do when you do get the text, and the buildup to this potential next date will be an emotional roller-coaster.

You can't stop emotions from arising. You're at work, the image of this person pops into your head, as does the question *Why haven't I heard from him or her?*, and your emotions kick in. What you do next is critical. If you give in to the emotions and get upset, your anxiety might drive you crazy for the rest of the day. But if instead, you push all such thoughts out of your head and concentrate on your work, then these emotions will quickly dissipate. And if you've kept your emotions on an even keel all week, then when that text does come in, you'll be much calmer. If that text doesn't show up, then you'll be able to forget about him or her much more easily.

The Dr. Ruth Method of Dating is to take action and then move on. Send that text, so you quickly deal with the question of whether you should text first or let him or her text first. You can then see what happens and get on with your life.

With each subsequent date, the emotional level is going to heighten, so if after five dates this person suddenly stops communicating, you're going to be much more emotional. There's no preventing the emotions at that point, and you shouldn't stop them anyway. If a relationship seems to be developing, you need those emotions to keep the fires going. And if it ends suddenly, that you feel really hurt is to be expected also. After all, in terms of emotional damage, divorce is considered just less than having a loved one pass away, so as you go up the ladder of a relationship, a sudden rupture is going to be more painful. You can't hold your emotions in check forever. After a first date, though, keep a tight rein on your emotions in case the relationship doesn't develop.

And if you're not interested in this date, show some respect and let him or her know that you don't want to pursue the relationship. Do it as gently as possible, but don't just stop communicating. It's rude, and more importantly, mean spirited.

I'm often asked, "How many dates do I give X before deciding whether to go forward or move on?" The answer depends on what obstacles are holding you back. There could be many, but none of which you consider a deal breaker. Up until now I've been telling you to keep your emotions reined in, but if you're in one of these "I don't know what to do" situations, then my advice is to let your gut decide.

> **Dr. Ruth Westheimer** ✓
> @AskDrRuth
>
> Picking flower petals isn't a good method for making decisions.

Instead of racking your brains trying to make a rational decision, or picking flower petals or tossing a coin, stop thinking about this decision for a few hours and then just go with the first answer that comes to mind. Your emotional brain understands some factors better than your rational brain, and because your rational brain is stuck bouncing back and forth between yes and no, just let your emotional brain make the decision. Might that decision end up being a mistake? Could be, but that risk is always there. The point is that you don't want to be stuck between that rock and a hard place for long, so better to just head in one direction and accept the consequences. You might lose someone who would have been perfect, or you might spend months with someone you end up hating, but at least you'll be moving instead of stuck.

How do you actually measure this thing called chemistry? You can't, which is what can make it so frustrating. Chemistry is a feeling, and feelings are ephemeral and changeable too. But—and this is a good *but*—feelings can grow. Having some feelings for this other person is like a little spark. If you blow on it gently, it just might catch and turn into a roaring fire.

I'm going to reach into my specialty bag of tricks for a moment to give you an example that might help you better understand the concept. Over the years young people who want to know their sexual identity have often asked me whether they are straight or gay. Many of them want to be straight but are actually gay. In any case, what I advise them to do is see whether or not they can get aroused through a sexual fantasy of one sex or the other. If they find only sexual fantasies about the opposite sex arousing, then that usually means they identify as straight; if it's the same sex, then they identify as gay.

When you think of this person you've dated, do you become aroused? The chemistry isn't just sexual, although a sexual component definitely exists, which is especially true in the beginning of the relationship. If the answer to this question is no—he or she doesn't make your libido act up at all—then this person might become a good friend but not a partner.

You certainly find some people sexually attractive, even those you know aren't right for you, so as I said, this attraction is only an indicator, not a sure sign that this person should become a partner. But if you're not sure whether you and this other person have chemistry, checking out how you feel about him or her sexually, even if you're not ready to act on it, will at least give you some direction.

Another important component of this chemistry, in addition to sexual attraction, is love—that feeling that makes your heart go pitter-patter and your stomach tie itself in knots. Sometimes these feelings of love burst out and sometimes they take a long time to grow strong enough to be noticed. As with sexual attraction, you can fall in love with the wrong person, and that's usually harder to deal with, because you're more invested when falling in love than falling in lust. As they say, love is blind. You can miss obvious faults in someone because you've fallen in love.

Other ingredients to this chemistry include the following: being able to make you laugh, brightening your spirits when you're down just by being with you, working well together as a team when sharing a particular activity, and having similar tastes. However, you can also share these activities with someone who is just a friend. That's why you like to spend time with a friend, because friends stir up in you certain emotions that come from the preceding list. The difference is that you're not sexually attracted to a friend, and even if you say that you love this friend, that feeling is far different from being *in love*.

You can't judge chemistry if all the evidence you have is from online meetings. If you're feeling strong emotions about someone you've never met in person, such feelings should be chalked up to wishful thinking, like a crush you might have on a celebrity you've never met and never will. That doesn't mean that when you do meet in person the two of you won't click. You might and you might not, because to fully judge the chemistry between two people requires physical proximity.

If you don't believe me, think about the times when after reading every online review you order some product that became your number one object of desire, but when it is finally delivered and you open the box, you are disappointed. Until you held that object in your hand and saw how it worked or fit or whatever, you couldn't be 100 percent sure that it was something you really wanted, no matter how much you thought you did. And if an object that has a limited amount of qualities can disappoint you when faced with the real thing, imagine how something as complex as a human being might not meet your expectations.

You can't judge chemistry until you meet, but this person you dated doesn't have to send you over the moon on a first date, and you don't have to be in love with someone you went out with to want to continue to date. The question that confronts you is whether or not the potential exists for this friendship that is developing between you to grow into love.

Let me insert a cautionary note here. Say at one point in your life you were madly in love with someone. The emotions swirling through your body were quite strong and kept you from sleeping, eating, or doing your work. Having those feelings reciprocated was an amazing state to be in. But for most couples, it doesn't last at that heightened level. As time goes by, those intense feelings grow duller—though that doesn't diminish the relationship any. In fact, going through life with those intense feelings of love constantly distracting you would be difficult. But what if you're seeking those intense feelings in your next relationship, and this person you're dating doesn't arouse them in you? Does that mean that the relationship is doomed? Although it's possible, in general the answer is no.

If you don't have any chemistry, then move on. But if you have chemistry and sense that it has the potential to grow stronger, even if not to the highest level of intensity but possibly to the level enjoyed by most long-term couples, then don't give up on this relationship, because the chemistry hasn't yet reached that intense state. When you first get something new, maybe a new dress or video game, it can spark intense feelings of enjoyment, but after a while those feelings will wear off. That doesn't mean that you don't continue to enjoy the item.

A new person in your life brings you a whole host of good feelings. You have to judge that entire package, not just how intense a few of the emotions are. Some of these emotions are essential, like sexual attraction, but your next partner doesn't have to be the one who sparks the most flames in that part of your anatomy. He or she has to possess the right combination: maybe you don't think of this person as being as sexy as a past lover, but he or she makes you laugh more or feel less miserable because you're being treated better.

Don't compare lovers. I know that isn't always easy to do, and your brain is going to involuntarily jump into making some instant comparisons. At the very least, don't spend time comparing particular strengths or weaknesses, but rather force yourself to compare the whole person. Maybe previous partner X was a better lover, but you're not together any longer, so some reasons must have made X less than the ideal partner. By looking at each person as a whole, hopefully you won't have any regrets when it comes to the person you're currently dating, especially because no two people are ever identical, so each will have pluses and minuses.

What if you're dating two people and can't decide? Each has qualities that you like, but neither seems to stand out over the other. I can't tell you which one to choose, but I can tell you to choose one of them and quickly. My reasoning is that as long as you remain in limbo, neither relationship will get a chance to bloom. You'll be holding your emotions in check, you'll be making comparisons, you'll be feeling frustrated, and you'll also feel guilty as you juggle your schedule saying yes to one date offer and no to another.

I see no problem in being completely arbitrary when making this difficult decision. Go ahead and select one category and whichever person wins, that's your choice. Could be the taller of the two, the richer of the two, the better educated, the one with the bigger muscles or breasts. You just need a way to break this tie.

If you really can't choose, then flip a coin and continue to see one person and tell the other one that you've decided not to continue dating him or her. Saying goodbye will be better for that person because he or she can then get on with life, and it will be better for you because you'll be giving this other relationship a real chance to develop.

Even if this relationship crashes, you can never regret the decision. Doing so would be a total waste of time and emotional energy. You make your choice and see what develops. That's not to say that if the relationship you choose doesn't work out, you can't make a casual inquiry with the person you didn't choose to see if he or she is still available and interested in seeing you again, but you can't count on that. (Of course, the softer landing you create when ending that relationship, the better the chances that if this person is still single, he or she will respond positively.) But if you're having a difficult time deciding now, then better to decide and make a mistake than to let months slip by waiting for some sign from above as to whom to choose.

Returning to the premise of this chapter and determining whether the two of you have the right chemical reaction, you have to understand that this reaction isn't fixed. Even if you're married fifty years, sometimes you're absolutely furious at your spouse, and other times you're melting with affection for him or her. One would hope that at the beginning of a relationship there was a lot more good chemistry than bad, but perfect chemistry doesn't exist. This analysis of chemistry you're undertaking can only be a judgment call. And like umpires and referees who gather to decide the right call to make, you each have veto power. Each of your judgments counts equally.

You can look at this budding relationship at this point in two ways. One is the short term. Do you want to go on another date? If you've gone on two, three, or four already, and you're not 100 percent sure how it's going, why not go on another so that you can find out more about each other? The second way to examine the relationship is through the lens of the long term. If some facet of the relationship clearly points to it not lasting long term, then end it.

One reason standing in the way of making a decision might be sex. You might be at the point in the relationship where the possibility of going to bed with one another isn't unreasonable. Some people won't make a final decision about the worthiness of a potential partner until they know how compatible they are in bed. However, having sex is more of an investment in the relationship. Women, especially, are unlikely to have an orgasm with someone that they don't feel comfortable with, and men are more likely to encounter difficulties (erectile failures or premature ejaculation) in such situations. And if things don't go well in bed, and you weren't sure of where things stood between you, then having sex could spell the end of the relationship. I say don't sit on the fence when agreeing to have sex, but be clear in your own mind that you want this relationship to develop.

Can you have an accurate reading of the chemistry between the two of you without having had sex yet? What takes place between two people during sex is certainly part of their chemistry, but what's important when judging chemistry is to have the desire for sex, not necessarily to have had sex. Just because you want to have sex with someone doesn't mean you're ready to actually engage in sex. You can want to see someone again, in part because you find that person sexy, but you still want to explore the relationship a bit further before becoming intimate. If the relationship is going to develop, and if the chemistry is right, then you'll be having sex soon enough. (Unless your beliefs, religious or otherwise, require you to wait to have sex until marriage, which is fine too.) The closer you get, the deeper the relationship before having sex, the less importance will be attributed to any awkwardness that might occur while having sex. It can take two people a little while to get comfortable with each other in bed. The first time you have sex could be mind-blowing, but it could also be disappointing. If the two of you have a relatively strong foundation and you care for each other, then you can more easily work through such issues. But if you're more strangers than lovers, any failures when having sex might put an end to the relationship, which might not have been the case had you waited.

Even though sex is likely to be better the deeper the relationship, the reverse may also be true. If you want a sexual episode to go well, especially if it's your first time together, then you might worry about the outcome to such a degree that those worries will interfere with your success. For example, a man who really wants to have a rock-hard erection may discover that his strong desire will also introduce the possibility of failure. If that concern distracts him, in turn it might then cause his erection to fail. If two people are in love, eventually they'll get over whatever problems such jitters may cause; however, if the relationship is a tenuous one, failure in bed could easily bring the relationship to an end.

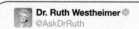

Dr. Ruth Westheimer
@AskDrRuth

Anticipation adds to the excitement of sex.

Having sex with a new person is always more exciting. No two lovers are the same, and not knowing what is going to take place or how you'll feel heightens the experience of that first time. Anticipation will add to your pleasure, but those strong initial feelings of anticipation disappear after you've had sex. You can only have sex for the first time once, so learn to enjoy that period before you have sex, appreciate the anticipatory sensations, and use any waiting period to strengthen the relationship. If the relationship goes up in flames or never ignites before you have sex, so be it. At least, you won't regret having had sex with this person who in the end was disappointing in other ways.

I said earlier that you shouldn't judge the potential of a date based on just one factor, such as appearance, but other factors might stand out after a few dates that make going forward impossible. For instance, say this person is sweet and intelligent and makes you laugh but has awful manners. He picks his nose or she slurps her food. Some people could ignore a habit like this, but you can't. Maybe the first few dates you were willing to ignore this behavior, but the more you think about it, the more you find it unappealing. That's the good thing about dating: you're not bound to one another. If something about this person really gets on your nerves and you're sure neither of you can change, then move on.

I really wish I could tell you to let this person know why you no longer want to stop seeing him or her, but I know how difficult that can be, and more importantly, I don't know that it would have any effect. If this is a lifelong habit, would he stop picking his nose so as not to get rejected by someone else just because you told him about this problem? Possibly. But more likely not, and so most people who break up just keep the reasons why to themselves. It's sad, but that's just the way it is.

You can learn an important lesson from breakups. If someone no longer wants to date you, more than likely he or she isn't going to be completely honest with you when saying goodbye. At that point, you can blame him or her for the decision, telling yourself that he or she made a big mistake because you're perfect and leave it at that. Or you can take a closer look at yourself and see if you can spot the reason. And then if you think you know why, you have to be willing to change your behavior, which won't be easy either, but it may serve you well when you start dating the next person.

We should all be trying to improve ourselves throughout our life. I'm nearing 90 years old, and I still teach college. My reason is because I learn as much from my students as they learn from me. So after a breakup, I suggest you do some soul searching, not because you want to try to convince this person to come back because you're going to change, and not even because you don't want someone else to leave you for the same reason, though that should be part of the decision, but mostly because if you've spotted some weakness, you want to improve for your own personal growth.

5.

Gearing Up for Round Two, Three, and Four

Humans go through stages. We start out as babies who reach various milestones, including learning how to walk, at which point we are toddlers. As our motor and communications skills improve, we hit childhood, followed by the teenage years and then adulthood. Relationships have similar stages. First dates are almost always awkward; two or three dates later you're getting to know each other, but you're not really close. Until you have sex with another person, your level of intimacy has a ceiling. But just the way that some babies learn to walk before they hit their first birthday while others take several more months, relationships don't develop along a fixed path. And that uncertainty can be quite confusing. Are you making progress or have you hit a wall? Are you sure that you even want the relationship to develop further? Can you picture spending the rest of your life with this person you're dating? And while all these questions are swirling around in your head, you still have a busy life to lead.

Some of this process is in your control and some of it isn't. For example, you might want the relationship to proceed full steam ahead, but your date has his or her foot on the brakes. And how do you interpret that? Is it just the desire to go slow or is there a line in the sand that this person has no intention of crossing?

If you want a relationship to develop, like many people you're going to treat this relationship like a delicate flower, afraid that any rough treatment could cause all the petals to fall off. I said "like many people," because some individuals don't believe in beating around the bush, and if they're not sure about the other person's intentions, they will just ask. Nothing is wrong with this approach, but if this other person isn't sure yet, then the added pressure might push the relationship into a more precarious position. If he or she is hesitating, when forced to decide, he or she might take the safe course and say that he or she isn't ready to move forward. But if you nurture the relationship by keeping the pressure off, you might coax this person into more of a commitment.

"But Dr. Ruth," I hear some of you asking, "why do I have to coax this person? If we have some chemistry, shouldn't this relationship just go forward on its own?" Yes, and your next flight is supposed to take off on time, but what are the odds that it will?

Every once in a while I have to resort to my specialty, sex, to underline a point, and this is one of those times. I hear couples complain that they don't have sex enough, but at the same time they want the desire for sex to arrive spontaneously. When two people are first having sex, they both might crave it all the time, so it's easy to match schedules and spontaneous sex seems the norm. But after a time, and with busy lives, matching sexual appetites exactly can be difficult. More often than not, if both partners agree to engage in sex at a particular time, even without much of an appetite for it, their libido soon takes over and they enjoy the experience immensely.

Similarly, people see sex scenes in movies where both partners have simultaneous orgasms while in the missionary position and believe that's what should be happening in their bedroom. However, statistics show that both outcomes—a woman having an orgasm in the missionary position and a couple having simultaneous orgasms—are the exception and not the norm.

Although some ideals are nice to fantasize about, my point is that they may not be realistic. You don't expect your partner to actually be a real prince or princess, do you? If some extra care is required to keep that little flame from going out, just accept it and do what needs to be done. Should this potential partner be trying harder too? Sure, but if you turn this into a game of tit for tat, you're surely going to lose. Some people's heads are in the clouds, so the more practical people have to take charge, assuming they know what they want. But let me return to my mantra about not wasting time: you're not in total control of this relationship, and if your partner doesn't want to go along with your plan to advance the relationship, then you can do only so much. If you exceed what you feel is the limit of time you're willing to wait, then you have to have the courage to move on.

<u>Stop and Consider:</u> **Are you sure that you want this relationship to grow stronger?**

For a certain amount of time, not knowing the answer to this question is fine. Although an impatient person like me might only give this a month, others might allow up to six months. But to stretch the time to make a commitment, even a limited one, beyond whatever boundary you feel appropriate is a mistake. If nothing else, you're sending a message to this other person that you have the patience of a saint. Not giving him or her any incentive to commit, given all the swiping that takes place around you, leaves too much temptation in play. For example, if you can't expect that this person would remove all dating apps from his or her phone after six months, then there's a good chance you're wasting your time. Perhaps you're the one who is being indecisive. That's okay, but you have to give yourself the same deadline. If you can't decide after six months whether the person you're seeing regularly could be a steady partner, then you need to acknowledge that something is wrong.

Sometimes you just have to take a leap of faith. Making a mistake is okay, but it's not okay to sit on the fence forever. After you make that leap and after you give yourself permission to fall in love with this person you've been seeing, you should fall in love. If you don't, then it was a mistake and the relationship will soon be over. But if you allow yourself to fall in love instead of holding your emotions in check, you will hopefully be repaid many times over for this commitment. Six months should be enough time to hem and haw before jumping.

You could also jump the other way—not into this person's arms but out the door. This is fine as long as you jump one way or the other. Staying put out of habit, or because you're afraid to be alone, or because you don't know what you'd say to your family and friends or post on Facebook is ridiculous. I know people do it, sometimes for fifty years, but I don't want my readers to fall into one of those situations. I want your love life to thrive, and for that to happen you have to take action.

How do you figure out where your relationship is after some set period of time, whether one month, three months, or six months? The first place to look is inside yourself. Could you be in love? Or is it just a wonderful friendship? How do you test for your chemistry? Here's one simple test. Make a list of everything that you like to do: go shopping, play tennis, read a novel, binge-watch a TV series, visit your parents, etc. Where on this list does being with this person you're dating fall? Be honest with yourself. I hope being with him or her is somewhere near the top, if not at the very top. But if the honest answer is somewhere in the middle, then you have some serious thinking to do.

6.

Ghosting and the New Rejections

Dr. Ruth Westheimer
@AskDrRuth

Dr. Ruth Tweets: Ghosting isn't scary; it's mean.

Ghosting occurs when someone you've been texting with suddenly stops answering. It also includes not answering phone calls and not responding to voice mails, e-mails, and every other type of communication, though it's most commonly used in regard to texting. You're not given a clue as to why your texts have made you persona non grata, and you're left to decide when the situation has become hopeless rather than the result of carelessness or rudeness. (It's not that ghosting isn't rude, but rudeness can be limited to a person just taking a lot of time to answer a text, while ghosting is a permanent halt to communications.)

Ghosting can take place at any point in a relationship. Maybe you've been texting for weeks but have yet to meet, or perhaps you've had one or more dates. It can even happen further along in a relationship. Whatever the backstory, suddenly this person disappears. (Well, that's not always exactly true, because on some apps you can tell that your text has been read, it just hasn't been answered. That can feel worse, but at least you can't blame the lack of response on some technical glitch.) Because e-relationships are easier to start, some people feel that these types of relationships should be easier to end. Even if you've met with somebody, you aren't guaranteed that just because you spent some time together, you had a clear road map as to whether the relationship was going to go forward or fall off a cliff. It's hard to say, "Sorry, but tonight's date is the last" to someone's face, so more often than not people put off communicating that they no longer want you in their life. But at some point you're given the message of rejection, even if it's just by a string of excuses not to get together. With ghosting, it's the cessation of all communications that's the bearer of bad tidings. You wouldn't have sent those texts if you'd known they wouldn't be answered, so you're completely blindsided.

What is particularly galling about ghosting is that answering a text takes so little effort. When someone just refuses to spend a few seconds typing a reply, that's a real slap in the face. They're conveying, without saying it directly, that you're just about completely worthless. The ghoster could also just be a big chicken, without the nerve to tell you goodbye. Either way, this behavior shows that the person doing the ghosting has no manners and, therefore, wasn't worthy of you. As bad as ghosting is, it also has a positive side, because the longer the "relationship" between the two of you had lasted, the more time you would have wasted on someone who is a boor. The only thing I can say to someone who has been ghosted is to forget about the ghoster as quickly as possible because he or she wasn't worth your time.

Since you don't know right away that you've been ghosted, days or a week or even more might go by without you knowing what's going on. You may think that this person never saw your text, which certainly happens when you get so many texts every day. Perhaps the wireless company screwed up and your text never arrived. Of course, the cause might be something not under the person's control, like an illness (though a check of his or her Facebook page or Twitter stream might tell you whether he or she is gone off the grid entirely). Left with all these unanswered questions, you're tempted to send a new text. But then you worry that sending another is going to seem as if you're stalking this person. And because you know that ghosting exists, you're going to think, *Am I being ghosted or is something else going on?*

To deal with ghosting, I suggest you develop a policy. After a specific period of time, say two days, of not getting a response, send this person a text that says you sent a text and maybe it never arrived, in which case please let you know. Otherwise inform them that when someone fails to reply to one of your texts after three days, you won't reply to any texts sent to you, thus giving him or her a twenty-four-hour notice. This rude person probably won't care that he or she can no longer text you, but you'll have the satisfaction of knowing that you were the one who cut off communications. Right after that, you have the job of forgetting about this person as quickly as possible.

Whatever you do when caught in a ghosting situation, don't spend days being angry. When thoughts of this rude person enter your head, push them out as quickly as possible. If one of your friends asks you about this person, just say, "I decided I never want to have anything to do with him or her" and end the discussion. If you spend time being angry and talking about this incident with your friends, you're only making the situation worse. You're adding to the impact of the ghosting, and why would you want to do that? You can be angry the moment you discover what's happened, but don't let your anger drag you down. Shrug it off and go on with your life, so that the effect of being ghosted is minimized, not maximized.

Another reaction that can take place under the dating umbrella is benching. In benching, you keep up sporadic communications via text, but for the moment you're really not interested, so you send this person "to the bench." If you take into account my feelings about time, then you won't be surprised to hear that to my way of thinking, benching may be worse than ghosting. With ghosting, you know that all interest has been dropped, but with benching, the person being benched still has some hope. And if he or she counts on that hope, that might cause that person to waste a lot of time waiting around for the relationship to resume.

If you're a veteran of using these apps, you may not invest enough of yourself in any of these relationships to worry too much about them. But I've spoken to people who've gone on lots of dates through an app and then find themselves in a quandary. One young woman's analysis of the current state of her relationship was that she wasn't sure whether she'd been benched or she was benching him. If I were in her situation, I'd send a goodbye text and get on with my life—if there's that much doubt in the relationship about each other's feelings, then those feelings weren't very strong or worth holding on to.

If you get only one date a month from these apps, your situation is far different than someone who goes out on an app date three times a week. If you're dating a lot, you might not even notice that you've been ghosted or benched. But if dates are rare, then not knowing what is going on in the head of someone you recently dated can be quite painful. Writing this person off would be a significant reduction in your dating pool, so the severity of the effects of ghosting and benching change, depending on the victim.

<u>Stop and Consider:</u> Would you be hurt if you were ghosted or might you not even notice?

When the only way to set up a date was by a telephone call, people often would sit by the phone hoping that it would ring. Although *ghosting* and *benching* may be new terms, they're not new aspects of the dating scene. What online dating has brought are methods of inflicting pain that didn't used to exist, and some of them are inherent to the way text messaging works. For example, if you and a friend are planning to get together later that day, your responses are probably going to be instantaneous. That's the nature of text messaging; it's much like a phone call after all. Unlike a phone call, when you're both on the line and talking to each other at the same time, there can be delays in responses to texts that can stretch seconds to minutes to hours to days. Those delays are going to cause you anxiety, because they'll give your mind time to wonder what's going on to cause the delay and whether communications will ever be reestablished. That's especially true if the text you're waiting for is from someone you're interested in romantically.

Another aspect of texting is that people will say things in a text that they wouldn't in a face-to-face conversation; this is particularly true when the subject is sex. If the person isn't standing in front of you, you're likely to be more open. That openness can include nude photos or sexting. Because some people get a thrill, to the point of orgasm, from showing off their genitals, if you meet a lot of people online, chances are that you're going to see some naked body parts. I'm not one to be a prude about nudity, and if you're no longer a kid, you're probably not going to be traumatized by receiving a picture of a naked person on your phone. But this sort of behavior certainly shows a lack of seriousness, unless you're at the point of the relationship where you're being sexual; therefore, after you receive such a picture you know that the relationship, whatever it was, is over, because this person's attitude toward sexuality is too immature to suit your tastes.

Unfortunately, some people look at ghosting and sexting as a sport. In all probability they aren't in a relationship and would have difficulties finding someone with whom to build a relationship. They're angry and bitter at the opposite sex. But what they can't do in person—attract a partner—they're able to do electronically. Because they're afraid of being rejected if they ever met in person any of the people they've met online, their entire goal is to hurt them, and what better way than to ghost or sext them?

Because such people exist, you have to be on your guard. You can't allow your emotions to get ahead of the state of the relationship. If you've never met, then you have to assume the relationship can't progress beyond its infancy. You can't risk falling in love with someone you've never met, because even though you've been communicating with a real person, he or she may have been playacting, so that the person you think you know may not even exist.

Dr. Ruth Westheimer
@AskDrRuth

Keep your heart locked up tight until you actually meet.

Some couples do start out in a long-distance online relationship and fall in love before they meet. If two people have gotten to know each other, especially if they're using an app like FaceTime or Google Duo to hold video chats, then getting to know someone fairly well after a few months of such communications is possible. You're seeing facial expressions, and if you've spent that much time staying in contact, then you have to assume that any stated emotional commitment is real. But such long-distance relationships are a bit beyond the scope of this book. In any case, that chemical reaction I've been speaking of won't fully take place until you're physically together, so use caution no matter how much it appears that the relationship is real.

As I said earlier, telling someone to his or her face that you want to end the relationship or that it never really existed can be difficult. But is passing on such news via a text really that terrible? Older people might think it rude to end a relationship in that manner, and if it were a long-term, serious love affair, then I would agree completely. But if you've gone out on a few dates and you decide that you don't want to go out on any more, then send a text that says so, in the nicest possible way, because if you don't like being ghosted, then you shouldn't ghost others. Here are some possibilities of what such a text could say:

> I enjoyed the time that we spent together, but I've decided that we're not a good match.

> It was fun, but it's over.

> Best of luck with the rest of your life.

> Sorry, but I don't believe that we're a good fit.

You could also tell a white lie. A white lie is told to avoid hurting someone else's feelings, so if you tell someone you've had a couple of dates with a former partner that is back in your life, he or she will understand that you two won't be getting back together but will take it less personally. Be careful with white lies, because if this person has other ways of checking, say through mutual friends, then he or she can easily learn the truth.

When saying goodbye to someone you've dated a few times, you might be tempted to explain more, including telling this person why you no longer want to see him or her. For example, if this person talks too much about him- or herself or constantly makes crude jokes, passing on your opinion may seem logical so that this person has the opportunity to change. The problem with such a tactic is that someone you're saying goodbye to probably isn't going to listen to your advice. He or she is going to be upset and angry; telling this individual the reasons that you don't want to continue the relationship will only make your message more painful. If you've had a long-term relationship with someone who, over time, you have said needs to change in some way, then maybe you could reinforce your advice on parting, and not through a text. But when it comes to someone you really don't know all that well, keep your thoughts to yourself.

As to my opinion on benching, although I understand the practicality of keeping your options open, it's important that everybody understand what is going on, which doesn't always happen. Most of the time the person sitting on the bench has no idea. If you get a text saying, *Sorry, I'm really busy, hope to see you soon*, you're going to feel that there's more hope than there might actually be.

And then you have to answer the question of how many people you keep "on the bench." Are these bench sitters ever likely to get in the game? Or is the person putting people on his or her bench playing a game, trying to collect the biggest bench?

If you suspect that you've been benched, don't just sit there, but instead force the issue. Push to see this person, even if only for a quick cup of coffee. If he or she can't even spare that much time for you, then assume that the relationship is over and don't bother answering those occasional texts meant to keep you on the hook. Your time is too valuable, and you need to concentrate on the other people out there who might actually want to be with you. If this individual asks to see you at some point in the future, then you can decide whether you want to do so.

By the way, I use this advice not only for romantic interests but also for business interests. If I want to see someone important and I really need a quick answer to a question, I leave word that I'm not looking for a lunch or dinner but just want to stop into their office for a few minutes. And it often works. I not only get the appointment, but if I'm asking for funding for some charitable project, I get the donation too. I've respected that person's time, and so he or she is more likely to be charitable to me. I don't pretend to be so important that other people should open a large block of time on their calendar for me. They might do so, eventually, but I want their answer immediately, so I find it better to ask for less time but at the earliest possible moment!

In dating, text messages don't always give you the answer that you need. Sometimes you need to see someone face-to-face in order to figure out whether the two of you have any potential to go forward. If you can't get that brief encounter, then you have to accept how low on this person's totem pole you are and move on.

Stop and Consider: Are you on somebody's bench?

Should you ever put someone on your bench? Only if there is any significant potential that the relationship could develop. Say you meet someone and you get along; the relationship has some potential, but you would prefer somebody else who is about to come back into the picture. Putting the first person on your bench for a short time would be excusable, because if the preferred person doesn't work out, you then would be willing to date the bench player. In other words, don't put people on your bench just to have some bench players. Dating isn't a game, because real people's real feelings are involved. If you do put someone on the bench and in a few weeks know for sure that you're serious with someone else, then let the bench player know. Do unto others and all that.

Benching isn't cheating, because there isn't much of a relationship in the first place. However, some people use benching as a way of cheating. They decide that this concept validates unacceptable behavior. If you were under the impression that you were a couple and suddenly you're being benched, don't allow the relationship to resume, no matter how tempted you are. Why? Because this other person clearly doesn't have the affection for you that you thought, and because if it happened once, it's likely to happen again, so resuming the relationship would be a no-win situation for you. After a certain line has been crossed in a relationship, such as there have been more than just vague indications of affection for each other, benching behavior isn't acceptable and should only lead to a breakup.

Nobody likes to be rejected because it's always painful. But there is a bright side to rejection, at least from my point of view. After it's settled that you and this other person aren't going forward with your relationship, no matter how meager or strong the bonds were, you're free to move on. Being in limbo is a waste of your time. As I've stated, time is your most valuable asset, so the sooner you're rid of this other person, the better. You may have wanted the relationship to go forward, but if it has to fail, it might as well be sooner rather than later. Feeling grateful for any kind of breakup is difficult, even if all you were doing was texting each other, but there is definitely a silver lining, so you might as well hold on to it.

7.

How to Know When You've Become a Couple

We agreed at the beginning of this book that the goal of dating was to become a couple with someone else. How do you know that you've reached that point? If he offers up a ring and she accepts, then the answer is obvious. But many an offered ring has been turned down, and some brides and grooms have not finished their walk down the aisle, bolting instead, so the deal isn't sealed until it is. I'm not limiting this potential for breakup to marriages; committed relationships are included.

Because there are now two of you, each of your responses is equally important. If you're madly in love and he or she is only mildly in love, then you have a problem. But notice the phrase *madly in love*—it includes the word *mad*, as in crazy, and sometimes this emotion is an unreliable indicator. Traits that might make your heart flutter today might not have lasting value, so you really have to examine the other person carefully before you give yourself permission to say he or she is the one for you.

Without nitpicking, because nobody is perfect, look at the faults of this love of your life. Can you live with him or her for the rest of your life? Or are you thinking that you'll get him or her to change? If the latter is the case, you're in for a rude surprise. Most people can be nudged to change a little, like not leaving the toilet seat up, but not in broader ways. I'm not saying that getting an alcoholic, for example, to overcome his or her addiction is impossible, but such an effort is more likely to fail than succeed. If you're already married to someone with a major flaw, then you might have to learn to live with it, but at this point you haven't yet said any vows, so think carefully about what life may be like in the future.

You're not perfect either. What's your weakest trait? And is this person capable of dealing with it for years to come? If he or she is constantly complaining about something you do regularly, then maybe that complaint is going to turn into a weak link in the chain. If you're sure that you can't alter your behavior, then maybe you have to face the fact that you're not meant for each other.

However, say that you're basically compatible. What about your relationship makes you think it can last forever? (Even if you haven't discussed marriage but only discussed moving in together, you're both admitting that you don't see an end in sight.) If you look at a couple as a team, important qualities that will advance the relationship—in addition to love and sexual attraction, which don't normally play a part in a sports team's cohesion—are being able to work well together, being tuned into each other so that you can understand each other without necessarily having to say anything, and being willing to sacrifice for each other and for the good of the team.

<u>Stop and Consider:</u> Are the two of you good teammates?

Are you two a team most of the time or only once in a while? You don't have to be teammates twenty-four seven, because you do have separate lives and should have separate interests. Having your own identities is healthy for the team, because if you spend every waking moment doing everything together, you're likely to get bored. You each need to bring in new stimuli that you gather in the outside world for the team to thrive.

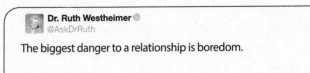

Dr. Ruth Westheimer
@AskDrRuth

The biggest danger to a relationship is boredom.

Boredom is the biggest danger any relationship faces. I'm not talking about sexual boredom, which isn't good, but it won't necessarily be fatal to a relationship. Some people have fallen into using certain methods or rituals over the years that they absolutely require in order to have an orgasm, so variety just won't work for them. It may not be an ideal way of having sex, but couples with a good relationship can usually overcome this type of obstacle. However, if the two of you are having dinner and find you have nothing to say to one another, that's a big problem. Good communications are critical to any relationship, but you need something to communicate about. Does she have to care about football and he about fashion? No, as long as they both found some topics are stimulating to their brains. To do so, cultivate those subjects and go out of your way to find activities that you can share and then talk about, which will then create a strong foundation for your relationship.

One factor that creates a team is having children; after having one or more, the couple becomes a team of parents. Parenting has many wonderful aspects, and working together to raise children is rewarding. But children grow up, and some couples discover, after the children have left the nest, that the only topic they had in common was the children. Without the children being front and center, nothing is left to hold the relationship together. Although you might not be anywhere near that stage, I raise what is called empty-nest syndrome as a warning flag of what can go wrong when a lack of communication exists. Believe it or not, most of the time the damage to a couple's relationship that is evident during empty-nest syndrome is irreparable. The slow disintegration of the relationship needed tending much earlier so that it never reached a critical degree. If you're more like two strangers than two close friends, even if you have some real passion at times, then maybe you're not right for each other in the long run. Maybe the drip, drip, drip of negativity will eat away at the core of the relationship so that at some point it reaches a breaking point.

<u>Stop and Consider:</u> What does the present state of your relationship indicate its future will be?

I bring up this topic because before talking to this boyfriend or girlfriend about your potential future together, you better be sure of how you feel. If you have doubts, then first make sure to sort out your feelings in your own head. I'm not saying that talking about certain aspects of the relationship with your lover will or won't pay off. But just as I discussed dating goals earlier, you need to have some goals or minimums in mind before you talk about where your relationship is heading. For example, your partner's been daydreaming about going back to college to get a degree for as long as you've known him or her. If you're working, then you'd be supporting this effort financially, at least to some degree. Is that something you'd even consider doing? If not, then before you could agree to further cement your relationship, you have to know that your partner's dream is nothing more than that.

<u>Stop and Consider:</u> What would the deal breakers be when you sit down to talk about your future together?

One reason this type of conversation is so scary to begin is that even though you've been dating for a while and everything seems perfect, at the end of the day, when you sit down to talk, you might learn that your partnership is not meant to be. Maybe this boyfriend or girlfriend of yours really doesn't want to stay together and hasn't figured out how to tell you. Or one or more deal breakers loom over the relationship. Or, as happens all too frequently, one of you wants a commitment and the other isn't willing to make one—maybe not now, maybe never.

<u>Stop and Consider:</u> What are your end-game goals?

Just because someone isn't willing to commit to a relationship or marriage, it doesn't necessarily mean the end of the relationship. Whether it does or doesn't depends, from your point of view, on the goals you've set. If a commitment is important to you and the other party isn't ready to take that step, you have to decide what to do next, which might depend on the nature of your partner's unwillingness. Does it lean more toward "not now but maybe later" or "probably not though you never know"?

What often happens in these situations is that one party sets a time limit, which may be communicated to the other or just set internally: *I'll give him or her three/six/nine months.* If you've invested a certain amount of time with this lover and you're basically happy, then not throwing it all away just because he or she won't agree to commit when you first ask about it makes sense. Staying together certainly saves you from having to endure the pain of a breakup. But what if that commitment is never forthcoming? If you're inevitably going to break up, you'll have wasted those added months.

You have to look at this lack of willingness to commit as a flaw, either in the relationship or in the other person. Each of you and the relationship undoubtedly have flaws, but possibly adding this flaw—a lack of willingness to commit—could or should be the breaking point. Because you can't expect perfection, you have to base your decision on a cumulative total of the pluses and minuses. And I'd tell you to consider it a major flaw when after a considerable length of time, your partner won't agree to a commitment.

Breaking up is hard to do, and it takes some time to prepare yourself to come up with a game plan. Just because this conversation about the state of your relationship doesn't go the way you had hoped it would doesn't mean the relationship is going to end then and there. It's not realistic for you to have this conversation, have your partner say he or she can't commit, and then just announce that you're leaving. But, if you're going to give this person a set amount of time to come around, you can't just pretend that everything is normal. You have to use that ticking clock to your benefit as well. You need to prepare the way for the breakup. If it doesn't come, great. If he or she says, "Yes, let's make our arrangement more formal," that will make you delighted. But if nothing has changed during this waiting period, then that period will have been a waste of time. If, on the other hand, you've laid the groundwork for a breakup, then the time between this conversation and the actual breakup will have been well spent.

This preparation will be both mental and physical. The mental preparation is the harder part, but the physical will make it easier. What do I mean by "physical"? Doing actual things, like making a list of all the activities that you like and your partner doesn't, and planning on how you're going to do as many of these activities as possible right after the breakup, so that you have something to look forward to. The mental preparation means trying to look as realistically at your situation as possible. Don't gloss over your partner's faults, as you normally might, but see how they've affected you, which will help you steel yourself in case the breakup does occur.

But I've gotten ahead of myself because I'm telling you what to do if the conversation doesn't go the way you had hoped, and I haven't given you any advice on how to actually have that conversation.

My first piece of advice about such important talks is to give a lot of thought to the locale. The best place to have it is while on a walk down a quiet country road. Why do I feel that way? A conversation like this is going to cause your adrenaline to spike, so your heart might be racing a bit and your breaths might come a little more quickly. Walking will decrease these effects, because your body will use some of that extra adrenaline to move your muscles. Such a hormonal reaction is part of the fight-or-flight response, so if you're walking, you're "fleeing" to some extent, which will calm you down and might help prevent this discussion from turning into a huge fight. If the two of you are in a closed room, some of that urge to flee will be present and that energy might be redirected into fighting, which won't be conducive to a positive conversation.

I said "quiet country road" because you want privacy. If you're lucky, this road will be away from any cell phone towers! You want to avoid interruptions, especially at key moments, which is why I don't suggest having such a conversation at a local restaurant, where the waitress may come over to ask you how you're enjoying your burger, or where the people at the next table might be eavesdropping. You want to be able to be honest with each other, which requires that other people aren't listening in, which might make you or your partner react differently for appearance's sake.

If you end up having this conversation in your home or your partner's, don't do it in the bedroom. Keep the bedroom, the main place where you have sex, a bit sacrosanct. That's why I advise people not to have a TV in the bedroom. If this conversation turns into a fight and yet you end up staying together, you don't want those bad memories of this fight or any other one creeping into your head every time you're in there.

I favor planning ahead for such a conversation. It may not be the first time you've discussed the idea of commitment, but catching your partner unaware when you want a well-thought-out response probably isn't a good idea. Let your partner know you want to have a serious discussion about your future, that you need to set aside some time, and do just that. This way he or she will have an opportunity to think about the issue, work out in his or her mind what the decision should be, and then reveal his or her true feelings rather than be blindsided by such a conversation and blurt out something that both of you might later regret.

What if your request for this talk is turned down because "we've talked about this a million times and you know how I feel"? That response will tell you a lot, of course, but insist on making this date to talk and then be ready to state your case, which might be, "If you don't want to commit, I can't stay with you." I'm against making threats. And I'm not suggesting that you should say this in order to get your partner to change his or her mind. But you have to be truthful, and you want your partner to understand how you really feel. Assuming that you'll leave if you can't get a commitment of some sort, then it's okay to say so, whether or not your partner perceives it as a threat. Of course, if you don't get that commitment, you do have to part ways. Just don't threaten to leave, especially in anger, if you don't really mean it.

There are degrees of commitment. The most basic is promised monogamy and the most advanced is marriage. Some people get stuck in between those two extremes for what seems like forever. The excuses tend to be about matters outside the relationship—for example, waiting to get the right job, pay off a loan, or finish a degree. Although these excuses can make sense, they also don't, because if two people are married, they're going to encounter turbulence and hurdles in their lives from time to time. If they're a loving couple, they'll actually be helping each other to get through them. Whatever job you have when you marry probably won't be the only one you'll ever have, so the decision to commit to one another shouldn't depend on an external factor like a job. If one of you has a parent dying of cancer who needs your help daily, that is something that might make a person not want to commit until the situation is resolved. Even in that type of situation, you both are going to be sharing this burden, so is this type of excuse entirely valid? Not wanting to set a wedding date with a parent dying is understandable, but not being able to set that date soon after this issue is no longer on the table might not be reasonable.

People are getting married later and later, and many aren't getting married at all. There's less societal pressure to get married, because unmarried couples can easily move in together, sign a lease, and even buy a house together. Because people are living longer, does it make sense to tie yourself to one person for fifty or more years? And with so many marriages ending in divorce, people easily use the excuse that marriage isn't permanent in any case. Although all that is true, an open-ended commitment is just that, open ended. Yes, you can question the point of getting married, but you can also question why you wouldn't want to get married. Why is there a need for an easy-out clause—to be able to walk away from a relationship without any consequences?

Having an exit strategy in your back pocket will prevent anyone from fully committing to a relationship. Every once in a while, after a rough spot in the relationship, you're each going to examine that exit strategy and consider what it would be like to use it. That reaction is only natural, but it also weakens the relationship. Every couple bickers from time to time. You have a right to your own opinions, and they won't always be in tune with your partner's, whether the issue is major or minor. The less commitment you have, the pull to walk away will get stronger, which in turn makes staying less likely.

Marriage settles things in both of your minds, which allows you to build from there. Sure, you can have kids out of wedlock, but when the going gets tough, and it will, can you count on your partner to stick with you?

Dr. Ruth Westheimer
@AskDrRuth

Dr. Ruth Tweets: Sharing your dreams will help build your relationship.

What about your dreams? You each have some goals for your own future, but reaching those goals in the arms of someone else who has been rooting for you will make them that much sweeter. Having dreams that you share, be it visiting some special place like Paris or Bali, owning your own home, or hiking the entire Appalachian Trail, will bring so much more satisfaction if you can make those dreams come true as a team. And if you have such a dream and you break up, now imagine going to Paris or hiking the Appalachian Trail alone and see how much you'll have lost.

I'm in favor of marriage, even after having had two failed marriages. In those two cases, I was probably wrong to get married, but I couldn't see it. I urge caution before you get that marriage license, but not so much caution that you don't take that final step.

What if you're not at the marriage stage yet but merely want to know that this person you've been dating won't be dating anyone else for the foreseeable future? Because a more casual relationship is on the table, it might not need as formal an agreement. But that doesn't mean that you are so casual as not to outline what you both feel will be the terms of the relationship. Certainly you both should delete any dating apps that you have on your phones. But do you give each other the right to inspect your phones at any time? If that's an issue, then what might one or both of you be hiding from the other?

This example illustrates the problem of not going all the way by getting married. When you're not married, there are going to be boundaries between the two of you. That you don't share a bank account might not be important, and yet the longer you go keeping such matters as your finances private, the harder it will be to open up if you ever do get married.

Here are some other topics to discuss openly. Birth control is certainly a topic to talk about rather than just assume each other's viewpoints and actions, as in he assumes that she's protecting herself. It may not be the right way of achieving this goal, but many women have allowed themselves to become pregnant in order to cement a relationship. Two people having sex need a lot of trust, concerning STIs as well as unintended pregnancies. Without that trust, some couples run into problems with their lives. For example, a man who isn't confident that his partner is taking her birth control pills may discover that worrying about that might prevent him from having orgasms during intercourse.

In the beginning of a relationship the male might be the one picking up the tab, but after a while that might become a heavy burden. Yet, a woman who wants to pick up the tab, especially if she makes more money, might come up against the male ego. Talking about financial issues, like who pays what and who contributes how much, could be vital to keeping the relationship going forward.

Don't forget to discuss the scheduling of your time together, which can be sticky. In the early part of a relationship, being together might take precedence over pretty much everything else besides the hours you have to be at work, but after a while you both need to find the time for other items like being with your friends and families. Some activities, like watching sports, might start to steal time away from one of you. If you're going to stay together, make sure you discuss this topic as well as the possible solutions. Deciding where to spend the holidays can be a minefield that's dangerous to cross. Rather than just playing it loose, when it's likely that one person will get hurt from time to time, work out your calendar so that it's as fair as possible to each of you.

One big advantage of having a commitment is that you can let your hair down in front of each other. After you've agreed to a commitment, you don't have to worry about what you look like when you wake up in the morning. I'm not saying that you should turn into a slob because you have a partner, but always having to be "on" when you're with someone isn't comfortable. Reaching the stage when you can have the confidence to not look your best in front of each other lessens the stress in the relationship and, therefore, in your life. Reducing stress is something that everyone benefits from.

Don't forget sex. Again, sex in the early stages of a relationship may just take care of itself, though that's not always true. If you're having any sexual problems, now would be the time to air them out. And by "now," I mean whatever point you're at in your relationship, assuming some sort of sexual activity is taking place. You should certainly be having some forthright discussions about sex if you already have a commitment, but that's also true if you're still waiting for that commitment. If she's not having orgasms and especially if she's been faking them, make sure you address this situation if the relationship is going to be even semipermanent. If he suffers from premature ejaculation, the couple can more easily find a solution if both of them work on it together.

Relationships have many components, and I look at sex as part of the glue that holds a relationship together. All couples cool off after a while in regard to sex, and married people often find that their deepening love fills in for the lessening of sexual intensity with regards to maintaining their relationship. But without a commitment, if the relationship is on shaky ground, the couple may have a harder time working through the stresses this cooling-off period can cause. One or both of you may start to think that the relationship is changing for the worse rather than just maturing.

Make sure you also discuss fighting and come up with rules of engagement. All couples have disagreements from time to time.

Getting married gives you a safety net of sorts, but you can't let the fight get out of hand just because it's with your spouse. But if you're not signed on the dotted line, you have to be careful with what you say. The relationship is more fragile, and too intense a fight could cause permanent damage. People also have different styles of fighting. If one partner comes from a family where loud shouting was the norm and the other person doesn't, what one would consider a relatively mild fight might seem all too intense for his or her partner. In order to limit the potential damage from disagreements, you need to work out some sort of playbook on how to handle arguments and fights so that their damage is limited.

This conversation on where the relationship stands is a complicated one. Even if you both agree to stand still and to make no promises of any kind, if you also are working under the assumption that you're going to stay together for the foreseeable future, then you have to talk about the issues I've just discussed. They're going to have an impact on your relationship, and so if you fail to address them properly, slowly but surely you'll start to drift apart.

And hanging over all these conversations—because it will probably take more than one to cover all the bases—will be this question of whether the two of you are a permanent couple or not. Even if you've agreed to put off that discussion, it will be impossible not to think about it. If neither of you wants to make such a final commitment, you're still going to wonder about the future and whether you'll be together. At this point you're romantically involved, you have strong feelings for one another, and you can't really imagine those just disappearing.

You could, of course, just jump to the conclusion that you'll stay together, with or without the paperwork, and operate on that basis. Plenty of couples have lived together for years, even decades, without formalizing their relationship. That's an option, but is it an option that you find acceptable? If you don't have a more formal agreement and you're going to insist on one at some point, then that puts a time limit on this current status. And that has to be said, even if the timetable is left blank. Offering a completely open-ended time frame is going to gnaw at you, assuming you're the one who wants to set some sort of date. In that situation, start some sort of clock ticking so that both you and your partner are aware that the current situation can't last forever.

Final Thoughts

I saw a video about two people who had met on Tinder and who then happened to be selected to receive a free trip together to Hawaii as a first date. It took them four years to finally agree to go on this trip, and that delay then became a news hook so that *Good Morning America* filmed their "date" and showed it on national television. This story of these two people represents one end of the online dating spectrum: those who are so highly selective (or such dawdlers) that before they'll agree to meet someone from a dating site, even with a luxury trip dangled before them, they might wait for what would seem like a ridiculous amount of time going on a date. On the other end of that spectrum are those people who go on five dates a week with people they meet through an app, not waiting for fate to drop someone into their lap but instead diving into the dating pool headfirst. And most people sit somewhere in the middle of this spectrum.

<u>Stop and Consider:</u> **Where do you sit on the dating spectrum?**

Is how often you date important? If you're not achieving your goals, either short or long term, then maybe frequency is part of the reason for how often you date. If you're not giving dating the priority it deserves in your life, then your dating goals may be further and further away. You can easily find excuses why it seems never the right moment to start implementing your dating goals. Sadly, many of these excuses aren't valid but really reflect an inner torment between wanting to find a partner and being afraid of the process. At the same time, if you date so much that you're not giving any one date the chance to prove him- or herself worthy of furthering the relationship, then that won't help you to meet your goal of finding a partner either.

If you chose to read this book, I can guess that you're not entirely happy with the way your love life is going. What I hope you now know is that there's no magic wand that I, or anyone, can wave over you to make the improvements you want, but instead you have to analyze your dating methods and habits, create a list of goals, and figure out how to meet them. And maybe the most important quality is persistence.

Do you know how Yoko Ono landed John Lennon? Once she met him, she proceeded to stalk him, standing outside his office, studio, or home in any weather. Eventually she was able to force Cynthia Lennon (his wife at the time) out of the picture. I could name many other famous couples where one wouldn't take no for an answer. I'm not saying pursuing one person so vigorously always works, but if you pour all your energies into your search for a significant other, then I predict you'll be successful. I can't give you a timetable, and maybe you can't be superpicky. Keep in mind that the best qualities that someone brings to a relationship aren't necessarily readily apparent. Qualities such as trustworthiness, faithfulness, a good sense of humor, dedication, etc. mean a lot more to a long-term relationship than appearance, social standing, or wealth. I urge you not to reject a string of potential partners based only on what you can see on the surface, especially from a brief glance at a picture on your phone. Instead take the time to dig a little deeper so that you can find a hidden gem.

Dating, if your aim is to get serious with one person, is difficult. Sure, some lucky people find a partner without much effort, but for every one of those people there are a lot more for whom finding that special someone is a struggle. In order to meet with success in the dating game, you'll need a lot of perseverance. Because most things that have value in this life require some effort to acquire, why should it be any different when it comes to locating that special someone who is going to bring such joy into your life? However, your search needs direction, or else you'll be wasting the most valuable asset you have: time.

That direction comes from having goals. With goals, of both the short- and long-term variety, you can measure your progress. Without goals you can flounder in the dating pool, even more so today than ever before. Before dating apps existed, the number of single people you might interact with was comparably small. Today you can swipe the pictures of thousands of singles, and that surplus of possibilities can make it harder to choose than ever before. Your goals can help you narrow the field so that you can find somebody to love sooner rather than later.

The older you are, the harder dating may seem today. Admittedly you never expected the changes that have come about to something as basic as dating, and it's going to take you a while to learn how to navigate these waters. You also have the experience to use older dating techniques, so having other resources to turn to might make dating easier. Finding that special someone will be a different kind of adventure than when you were younger, but in the end you might find it easier than before, not harder.

And no matter how old you are, if you've lost a long-term partner to a rival, Father Time, or the inability to hold the relationship together, dating has a different significance for you. You know what it means to share your life with someone, so you know what you're missing, which should drive you to wanting a replacement as soon as possible. You've also lost an important part of yourself, and that fear of being hurt again will affect your approach to dating.

If I've made one point over and over again, it's that dating is hard and sometimes scary. The rewards are well worth it, so when it comes to dating be like the turtle. Stick your neck out by swiping, going to events, telling everyone you know that you're looking for a partner, winking at strangers, and every other possible way you can think of. When you reach your goal of finding that special someone, the immense joy will fill your life so that you'll have no doubts that what you went through was a lot more rewarding than scary.

ACKNOWLEDGMENTS

Dr. Ruth K. Westheimer's Acknowledgments

To the memory of my entire family, who perished during the Holocaust. To the memory of my late husband, Fred, who encouraged me in all my endeavors. To my current family: my daughter, Miriam Westheimer, EdD; son-in-law, Joel Einleger, MBA; their children, Ari and Leora; my son, Joel Westheimer, PhD; daughter-in-law Barbara Leckie, PhD; and their children, Michal and Benjamin. I have the best grandchildren in the entire world!

Thanks to all the many family members and friends for adding so much to my life. I'd need an entire chapter to list them all, but some must be mentioned here: Pierre A. Lehu and I have now collaborated on two dozen books; he's the best minister of communications I could have asked for! Cliff Rubin, my assistant, thanks! Dr. Peter Banks; Simon and Stefany Bergson; Nate Berkus; Michael Berra; David Best, MD; Frank Chervenak, MD; Richard Cohen, MD; Martin Englisher; Cynthia Fuchs Epstein, PhD; Howard Epstein; Raul Galoppe, PhD; Meyer Glaser, PhD; David Goslin, PhD; Amos Grunebaum, MD; Herman Hochberg; David Hryck, Esq.; Steve Kaplan, PhD; Rabbi Barry Dov Katz and Shoshi Katz; Bonnie Kaye; Patti Kenner; Robert

Krasner, MD; Nathan Kravetz, PhD; Marga Kunreuther; Dean Stephen Lassonde; Matthew and Vivian Lazar; Rabbi and Mrs. William Lebeau; Robin and Rosemary Leckie; Hope Jensen Leichter, PhD; Jeff and Nancy Jane Loewy; John and Ginger Lollos; Sanford Lopater, PhD, and Susan Lopater; Rafael Marmor; David Marwell; Marga Miller; Peter Niculescu; Dale Ordes; Rabbi James and Elana Ponet; Leslie Rahl; Bob and Yvette Rose; Debra Jo Rupp; Larry and Camille Ruvo; Simeon and Rose Schreiber; Daniel Schwartz; Amir Shaviv; David Simon, MD; Betsy Sledge; William Sledge, MD; Mark St. Germain; Henry and Sherri Stein; Jeff Tabak, Esq., and Marilyn Tabak; Malcolm Thomson; Ryan White; Greg Willenborg; and Ilse Wyler-Weil. And to all the people at Amazon Publishing who worked so hard to bring this book into the world: Jeff Belle, Erin Calligan Mooney, Chad Sievers, and the entire team, as well as Amazon's founder and his wife, Jeff and MacKenzie Bezos, who, by inviting me to Campfire, launched this endeavor.

Pierre A. Lehu's Acknowledgments

Thanks to my wife, Joanne Seminara; my son, Peter; my daughter-in-law, Melissa Sullivan; my fantastic grandsons, Jude Sullivan Lehu and Rhys Sullivan Lehu; my daughter, Gabrielle; my son-in-law, Jim Frawley, and their adorable daughter, Isabelle. And of course, to Dr. Ruth K. Westheimer for allowing me the privilege of working on so many of her books.

ABOUT THE AUTHORS

Dr. Ruth K. Westheimer is a psychosexual therapist who sprang to national attention in the early 1980s with her live radio program, *Sexually Speaking*. She went on to have her own TV program, appeared on the cover of *People* magazine and *TV Guide*, and is the author of thirty-seven books. Fans of all ages can find her at www.drruth.com, on Twitter under the handle @AskDrRuth, and at www.youtube.com/drruth. A one-woman show about her life, *Dr. Ruth, All the Way*, is currently touring. Dr. Ruth teaches at Teachers College, Columbia University. She lives in New York and has two children and four grandchildren.

Pierre A. Lehu is a publicist, agent, and writer. He has written twenty-five books, including *Sex for Dummies* with Dr. Ruth, *Saké: Water from Heaven*, *Fashion for Dummies* with Jill Martin, and *Living on Your Own: The Complete Guide to Setting Up Your Money, Your Space, and Your Life*.